The Wicklow World *of* Elizabeth Smith 1840–1850

Elizabeth Smith (1797–1885) was born in Edinburgh but lived for more than 50 years in County Wicklow. For most of this time she kept a detailed personal journal in which she confided her frank opinions about contemporary events, as well as about people – politicians, profiteers and paupers alike.

The Wicklow World *of* Elizabeth Smith 1840–1850

Edited by
Dermot James and Séamas Ó Maitiú

THE WOODFIELD PRESS

This book was typeset in Ireland by Viskadal PS for
THE WOODFIELD PRESS
29 Oaklands Terrace, Terenure, Dublin 6, Ireland.

A catalogue record for this title
is available from the British Library.

ISBN 0-9528453-0-X pbk
0-9528453-1-8 cased

This book has been published with the assistance of
Wicklow County Council.

Printed in Ireland
by Genprint, Dublin

Contents

Illustrations

Preface

I have known West Wicklow since I was a teenager when I started to hike, climb, cycle and camp in this lovely area so close to Dublin's doorstep. Having a great liking for Scotland, I am also familiar with the central Highlands – especially the Cairngorms region where, over a long period of years, I usually based myself at or near Rothiemurchus. Yet, despite this familiarity with both of these areas, until three years ago I had never heard of Elizabeth Smith (née Grant) for whom these were the two most important places in her life.

Elizabeth Smith's father was the Laird of the vast Rothiemurchus Estate, and she married Henry Smith of Baltiboys House, a few miles from Blessington, which became her home from 1831 until the end of her life. I discovered all this and a great deal more from a book which I chanced upon and bought just a few miles from her Scottish home. She was, as I learned, a remarkable woman. She was well-travelled, extremely intelligent, observant and had a remarkably retentive memory. She was a very determined person, strict when needs be, yet compassionate and kindly. She was a good business woman, she was shrewd and had a wry sense of humour. Above all else, however, she was literate. In 1840, she began to keep an almost daily journal, recording in minute detail what was happening in her household, on the estate, around the neighbourhood and beyond. Andrew Tod wrote this of her in his introduction to her *Memoirs* which detailed her life before coming to Ireland:

> Her witty eye never fails to animate the manners, fashions, and events of her day; more than that her manuscript is an inexhaustible document of social and historical value.

This is exactly the point. Her journal, which has survived intact, is a social history of rural life in Ireland 150 years ago. Had she embarked upon her journal with publication in mind, she would have been much more circumspect about committing her candid comments to paper. This was not the case, however, and as David Black wrote in the magazine *Country Living*:

> She might have been another Regency gentlewoman had she not decided to write her memoirs .... These were essentially a private record of family life written for her children ... and were almost certainly never intended for publication, which was probably why she felt free to express hersef with blistering honesty.

Her Scottish *Memoirs* have long been recognised as a classic of nineteenth century Scottish literature and have been well-known and deservedly popular for about 100 years in the land of her birth. Sadly, her Irish *Journal* has never received anything like the same degree of recognition in her adopted country where she lived for more than 50 years. True, some scholars and historians have discovered her, quarrying her writings for quotable references to the Famine, and while this volume covers that terrible period, what she had to say abour all the other things that happened is, for today's reader, just as important and every bit as readable.

A representative selection of extracts from Elizabeth Smith's journal form the principal part of this book. Her punctuation has been altered where this appeared to make for easier reading, but her sometimes curious use of capital letters, as well as her spellings are faithfully followed throughout, including words like *encreasing, interiour* and *publick,* and also place names like *Blesinton, Baltinglas* and *Baltiboys.* Indeed, while the generally accepted spelling of the latter is 'Baltyboys', Elizabeth's rendering of the word has been followed throughout the linking text. Also retained are her renderings of certain Irish surnames, such as Commins, Doolen, Kiogh, Riley and Shehan.

Soon after the opening pages of Elizabeth Smith's journal, the reader is introduced to her family and friends, as well as to the tenants. Her children were three in number, Janie, Annie and Jack, then aged approximately ten, eight, and two, while she was 43 years old and her husband 61. When writing about her husband she sometimes called him 'Hal' but more usually he is simply 'the Colonel', and if the latter appellation seems rather formal, she occasionally referred to herself as 'Mrs Smith', though she was usually known as Eliza or Eli to her family. Throughout most of the main text in this volume, Mrs Smith is simply called 'Elizabeth'.

After Elizabeth arrived in Ireland, her sister Jane wrote: 'They have made an Irishwoman of you now, and may they know the value of the daughter they adopted into their country'. I think it is fair to say that they, or rather *we* in Ireland, have yet to recognise the value of this most unusual and interesting woman.

The aim of this volume is to redress this situation.

Acknowledgments

Throughout the several years involved in the preparation of this book, whether in correspondence, telephone calls, or in interviews, I have met with nothing but courtesy, encouragement and willing assistance so that the task has been one of unalloyed pleasure. My sincere thanks are due to everyone who responded readily and generously, but because listing them individually would make for tedious reading, I must content myself by mentioning the following.

My first debt is to Roderick Watson, who, as series editor of the Canongate Classics, Edinburgh, gave me every encouragement when I initially sought approval to quote directly from *The Highland Lady in Ireland.* I also owe a great debt of gratitude to the book's editors, Patricia Pelly and Andrew Tod for their permission to do so, and additional thanks are due to Patricia Pelly – a great great-granddaughter of Elizabeth Smith – who was so helpful with many suggestions and the loan of family material, and who also invited me to see the original manuscripts.

For their permission to use archive photographs, my thanks are due to the Head of the Department of Irish Studies at University College Dublin, and to *The Irish Times.* For permission to reproduce original matter, I am indebted to Matthew Stout whose cartographic skills are very evident in his three maps reproduced in these pages, and equally so to Maeve Costello, whose painting adorns the cover. In this latter connection I wish to acknowledge here the financial assistance received from Roadstone which made possible the production of the book's attractive cover. I remain to be convinced that there is anyone else in Ireland who knows more about Elizabeth Smith than Anne Denard. Anyway, she deserves special mention for her most invaluable help, not least in pointing me in the direction of little-known sources.

I consider myself exceptionally fortunate in finding, as my publisher, Terri McDonnell of The Woodfield Press, whose enthusiasm and expertise has proved invaluable in navigating the project through the turbulent and rock-strewn seas of book publishing. I am additionally grateful to her for introducing me to Séamas Ó Maitiú who, unknown to me, separately 'discovered' and researched Elizabeth Smith shortly after taking up residence in West Wicklow. His fascination with the people and places mentioned in the pages of her remarkable diary has led him to giving talks and lectures on both the journal and its author. Most of the photographs reproduced in this volume are his, and many of the other illustrations and a good deal of the background material are the direct result of his research, proving the point that it was a most happy chance that our paths converged during the final months prior to publication.

Dermot James, August, 1996.

Introducing Elizabeth Smith

Elizabeth Smith (née Grant) was born in 1797 at 5 Charlotte Square, Edinburgh, the eldest child of Sir John Peter Grant. Sir John's legal work meant that the family lived for the most part in the Scottish capital, but the long holidays were mostly spent at the family estate, The Doune, at Rothiemurchus, near Aviemore in the Highlands. Elizabeth's mother was Jane Ironside from County Durham, whom the majority of the then Gaelic-speaking tenants long continued to regard as a foreigner.

Elizabeth always regarded herself as a 'Highland Lady' and was immensely proud of her Clan Grant connections, and never lost her deep affection for the family seat, 'the dear home of all our hearts'. However, in 1827, The Doune abruptly ceased to be her home after her father found himself in financially straightened circumstances and brought the family out to India, where he had been appointed to a Bombay Judgeship. Elizabeth wrote in her Scottish *Memoirs* a hauntingly sad description of her final few days at the The Doune, and of her last walk with one of her sisters through the garden out into the woods and on to the nearby little loch, before returning around the hill and past the little estate church which overlooked the house. They had not intended going so far but felt drawn further 'enticed by the beauty of the day, the loveliness of the scenery, the recollections of the life from which we were parting'.

Shortly after arriving in India Elizabeth, who was then 30 and still unmarried, was introduced to Henry Smith, a colonel in the Indian Army, who came from Blessington, Co. Wicklow. At first the family teased her a lot: 'Oh you will so like Colonel Smith, Eliza, everyone likes Colonel Smith, he will make such a kind husband, he is so kind to his horses'. But it was not too long before the pair became engaged, even though Elizabeth's mother – who did not approve of any of her daughters' marriages – thought Henry Smith was 'no great catch, just a soldier'. Ten days before the wedding took place in Bombay Cathedral, word came from Ireland that Henry's bachelor brother had died and he had now inherited the family estate at Baltiboys, near Blessington.

The Doune: The mansion on the extensive Rothiemurchus estate in the Scottish Highlands, where Elizabeth's father, Sir John Peter Grant was Laird. (Dermot James)

Elizabeth and her husband arrived back in England in the Spring of 1830 and three months later their first child, Jane, was born. The baby was named after Elizabeth's mother and sister, and it was near her sister's home that they stayed until after the birth. Soon afterwards the little family at last set off for Ireland and, as Elizabeth wrote: 'Then, indeed, I felt I was gone out of my own kindred, and had set-up independently – a husband – a baby – and an end to Eliza Grant'.

Ten months in Dublin was enough to show the Smiths that town life was not suited to them, especially for Henry who suffered from asthma, and they resolved to settle down in Baltiboys where, as Elizabeth recorded, her husband would find: '.in his old neighbourhood all those companions of his youth whom he had left there more than thirty years before'. Furthermore, Baltiboys House, the ancestral home of Henry Smith, was in a ruinous condition, having been badly neglected for some 30 years so the Smiths lived in Dublin at 7 Dominick Street while they refurbished Burgage Cottage on their estate and considered what to do about Baltiboys House.

This was the state of affairs when Elizabeth's sister Jane and her husband, Col. Pennington, called to see them during their tour of Ireland in Autumn, 1831. Jane was almost as accomplished as her sister in observing and commenting on what she saw, and wrote a detailed description of that tour, including the reunion with her sister in Dublin and what she thought of the city before travelling to Blessington to see for herself the state of Elizabeth's future home. Some extracts from Jane Pennington's *Tour of*

Ireland, 1831, serve to complement this general introduction of the reader to Elizabeth Smith's background and circumstances immediately after her arrival in Ireland:

> I don't know how it is, but whenever I have been parted from Eliza for more than a month, she has, at our first meeting again, appeared more altered than most people do in the course of the years. I believe it is from her extraordinary propensity for falling in the ways, the habits, customs, manners and opinions even, of those she lives with; a faculty of extreme value to the possessor, as it is sure to endear her to everybody by whom she is surrounded, and fits her for every possible change of place or condition.... They have made an Irishwoman of you now, and may they know the value of the daughter thus adopted into their Country.
>
> I was annoyed to see Eli so thin, and to hear her talk so Irish. Colonel Smith has no brogue at all compared to her, and he is looking so much better than when he first landed from India that if I had not seen him between that date and this I should certainly not have known him. Nothing could exceed the warm kindness of his reception, expressed with every look as well as in his words of Welcome.
>
> Little Miss Janey [Elizabeth's daughter, then aged 15 months] is far too important a member of the family not to be noticed. In spite of a very soft and striking expression of countenance when she smiles, a complexion beautifully fair with pink cheeks, small features and glossy golden hair, she is not a pretty child. She stands, perhaps, a better chance of being a pretty woman. She is neatly made, and is both strong and healthy and full of intelligence....
>
> It was still early enough in the day for a stroll, and as the weather was clear and the streets clean – not often the case in Dublin – we all went out to walk a little about the town. We had entered it so suddenly, and reached our abiding place so at once, that we had as yet formed no notion of the general appearance of the town; and we were proportionately struck when a very few minutes from the Smith's door brought us into Sackville [O'Connell] Street. This is a very grand street indeed; so extremely wide, and the houses on either side sufficiently regular to keep the imposing appearance of height and size; and sufficiently irregular to save all that tedious, ill coloured formality and sameness that spoil the whole effect of the new town of Edinburgh. Sackville Street is not very long, and a statue [Probably Nelson's Pillar, completed twenty five years earlier] newly erected in the centre of it cuts off the vista as you look along it from the end; still, I think, it is the finest street I have seen.

Jane went on to admire the shops and some of the other fine streets and squares, and thought the houses around St Stephen's Green were the finest of all, describing them as 'really palaces'. She also commented on the number of 'military' moving about on foot and horseback, giving an air of life and gaiety which, as she said, not even London could match, but then added that 'one could not help associating in one's own mind their presence with the causes of it'. This was Dublin as the Smiths knew it, their temporary home until they were able to move to Blessington, and two days later they all set out so that Jane could see Baltiboys for herself. This is Jane's description of the journey to Blessington, which place she thought was 'remarkably clean and tidy looking for this part of the world, and has a smart Inn...'.

> It is about seventeen miles of very good road from Dublin to Burgage; not a mail road, but there are three Coaches upon it. About half way, there is a very long, stiff hill to climb – which is the more provoking as it might have been wound round with ease.
>
> From the top of this hill the view is amazingly extensive and extremely grand; Dublin I could only remark by its smoke; but the Bay is here seen to admirable advantage. Colonel Smith and I walked up this hill, after accomplishing which, we stopped at a little public house [probably at Brittas] to water the horses....We performed our little journey very well; it is up hill all the way.

The two couples then stayed for a few days in the recently refurbished Burgage Cottage, situated a short distance to the north-west of Baltiboys House, which Jane described in detail:

> I don't know that I ever slept under a roof so truly *cottage* as this Burgage. It is thatched, and has no upper storey to the front; though between, the Nursery and two other rooms are over the kitchen. But this taller building was not quite connected with the original house till now that Colonel Smith has built in the space between them, taking occasion, it seems to me, to add some closets and a man servant's room above them.
>
> The main house consists of four bedrooms, formerly a parlour on each side of the door, and a bedroom beside each parlour. The parlour on the right is a very good-sized room, and Eli has made it look exceedingly pretty by exertion of a little good taste in adding to the furniture – for it is by way of a furnished house. It is a much better height than from the outside of the house one would expect, but as there is nothing on the roof above it, there is more space than the eye gives credit for. The little dining parlour is not so good; the bedrooms

> are good enough; but I don't myself like sleeping on the ground floor.... The ground about the Cottage is pretty and, if improved and kept in order, would be extremely so. It is altogether unpretending, and for a cottage (with Colonel Smith's additions properly completed) will be comfortable and, then, it is close to Baltiboys...

The walls of Burgage Cottage can still be traced less than a quarter of a mile from Baltiboys House, hidden in the bands of conifers which fringe the present-day reservoir which has done so much to change the landscape here since Elizabeth Smith's time.

On the following day, Jane, accompanied by Elizabeth and her husband, drove the short distance from Burgage Cottage to Baltiboys House. Jane recorded that the scenery was more beautiful than she had expected and the River Liffey was 'a very significant streamlet' which joined the King's River so that Baltiboys was half encircled by the two rivers – just as it is today by the lake. Elizabeth later explained how they would sometimes take a short-cut from the cottage to see the work in progress on the big house by wading across the river 'Highland fashion'. Jane's description continues:

> We went over a bridge [Burgage Bridge], but I cannot remember which River it crosses; I think the Liffey. On a little hill near this bridge stands a ruined chapel and an old cross of considerable size cut out of one stone; so that some art must have been used to elevate it, unless it was carved out of the living rock. This hill is upon Colonel Smith's property. Having gone to the left to get to the Bridge, we now turned pretty sharply to the other hand, and soon reached an old gate; this let us into what ought to be the approach to Baltiboys. At present there is only a mere cart road; but which might easily be so converted as to make a very handsome avenue.
>
> [The house] is cut on the side of the hill, and the ground is to the right, sloping down to the King's River, is already planted; and the steeper part on the left will be done next. This terrace commands a fine view of all that the country has hereabouts to show, namely the river running brightly and in agreeable curves through level banks of very vivid green; a few clumps of trees where gentlemen's houses are situated; and some wild, but not high or picturesque, hills behind. The eye longs for more wood; and if people would only spend, I see no reason why all this should not become sufficiently interesting. For though, as I have said, the immediate banks of the river are low and level pasture lands where cattle graze winter and summer, there is no want of variety of ground beyond. As we drew near to where the old house of Baltiboys

Colonel Henry Smith, who unexpectedly inherited the family estate near Blessington ten days before his marriage to Elizabeth. (Patricia Pelly)

stood – a mere ruin now – we came upon good sized trees which, compared with other places in the neighbourhood, are in real profusion, and among them are some of handsome figure...

Eli and her Colonel have all the desire to plant more, whether they finally resolve to build at this place or not. It is now in a very curious state of abandonment. The house, I believe, was dismantled for the sake of selling the materials when the old proprietor determined to live abroad. But a great proportion of the walls are left standing, and cover a very considerable area; and with office and all, there are more than twice the quantity of stones that it would take to build a convenient mansion.

The grand point is to decide on the best site for a new house. Colonel Smith is fond of having it as near the old one as is consistent with a better view. He has some good reasons; the old trees, the old stones, and a run of water to supply the house are all at hand; the old garden too. A very little further along the terrace there is a nice open field sloping to the river, with a plantation of the sort of neglected kind I have described, behind. And one or two clumps in front that have grown more freely. This site commands by far the best view I have seen in Ireland, always excepting Newry...

The Smiths then drove Jane to see Pollaphuca Waterfall and the deep gorge into which the cataract used to fall until the new reservoir dam was erected in 1939. On seeing the cascade Jane wrote:

> This is the famous 'Pola fuoca' or Devil's Caldron, on the high road which one might pass along every day for years without guessing all that the hitherto stupid Liffey is doing among the rocks below. This fine cataract is the grand lion of this part of the country. The people come from all parts to visit it; great numbers from Dublin. The walks have been made with great judgement to shew it off completely and from every side. The tea room fronts it, of course, and with the generality of visitors, the view from its windows is the favourite one. The opposite bank is equally steep with that on which we were, but it is not wooded. The effect of the hill is highly pleasing, and very much raised my opinion of Nature's handiwork in this, her Emerald Isle. I hope one day to visit other scenes in Ireland of still finer character.

Elizabeth herself later described her first impressions of her future home, 'ruins – nettles – broken gate – road overgrown with weeds'. Her great-granddaughter, Edris Stannus, was much later to describe the house as a long, two storied building with a spacious network of basement rooms. It was a typical Irish country house of about 1820-30, late Georgian in part, consisting of one main wing and two smaller ones. Edris Stannus is much better remembered by her stage name, Ninette de Valois, the internationally famous ballet dancer and choreographer who wrote that description in her memoirs, *Come Dance With Me* (London 1957).

Elizabeth also described the chaotic state of the tenants resulting from her brother-in-law's neglect of the property. In a study of land-holding and population decline on the Smith estate, Matthew Stout shows that there were 30 holdings held by 28 individuals on the estate at the time of the Tithe Applotment Books in the mid 1830s.[1] As alluded to by Elizabeth a policy of consolidation followed, much of it in the pre-famine, indeed pre-journal period, and was continued over the famine years. When Elizabeth undertook her comprehensive visitation of all the tenants in January 1847 the number seems reduced to about 18 and Griffith's Valuation of the early 1850s lists 15 tenants.

The Smiths were a prominent family in the Blessington area going back to the early years of the eighteenth century at least, though family tradition has it that the Graydon Smiths are descended from a late thirteenth century Brian O'Grady who rebuilt the castle at Boystown (an earlier name for Baltiboys) in 1270. Records show that in 1719 a Joseph Smith of Balnabarney, County Kildare and John Smith of Miltown, Dunlavin, took out a lease on 674 plantation acres of Lower Baltiboys. This land had been

1. Matthew Stout, 'The Geography and Implications of Post-Famine Population Decline in Baltyboys, County Wicklow' in *Fearful Realities – New Perspectives on the Famine*. by Chris Morash & Richard Hayes, (eds.), Dublin, 1996.

in the hands of John Smith, lately deceased, and his undertenants, and the two above-mentioned Smiths were executors of his will; it is not stated how they were related to the deceased but they were in all probability his sons. This lease was granted by a Walter Harris of Dublin and Westmeath and Joanna Bradshaw of Dublin. As well as the land, it also granted 'liberty of cutting and getting turf out of the Bogg of Ballynehown for the use of the Mansion House of Baltiboys and three families'. It would appear, then, that there was a house on this site going back to the seventeenth century. The family rose to some prominence and two John Smiths of Baltiboys were High Sheriffs of County Wicklow, one in 1741, perhaps the John who had lived near Dunlavin, and another, more than likely Henry's father, in 1768. He died in 1790 and he seemed to have lived up to the reputation of the hard-drinking, hard-riding, devil-may-care image of eighteenth century Irish 'half-mounted gentlemen' as a family tradition has it that he jumped off the old five-arched Burgage Bridge one evening returning from a hunt ball.

* * *

Nine years after her sister's visit, Elizabeth Smith decided to keep her own detailed journal, a fascinating document which has survived intact, and which provides today's reader with her remarkably perceptive, contemporary glimpses of life in Ireland in the middle of the nineteenth century. The extracts used here are culled from her journals written between 1840 and 1850, and are all the more interesting because they were not originally written for publication and her views about everything and everybody are, consequently, remarkably frank – whether she was writing about Queen Victoria, the government, her gentry friends, her own family, or her humble and sometimes troublesome tenants. On at least one occasion she seemed to doubt the wisdom of writing so frankly:

> I have been thinking whether it has been quite right in me to set down, for evil as well as for good, in this written exposure of feelings which I intend to be read by my children, all my private opinions of people and people's actions, some of them very near and very dear to me. My tongue I know often goes too fast – my pen too, I suppose, for it runs on over the words just as the tongue does. However, dear children, you may just remember this that whether what I feel be wrong or right it is my honest impression at the time.

The views presented are, of course, those seen from the local 'Big House', but the picture that comes across very strongly is of a landlord and his wife who, while strict, were generally kindly in their dealings with their tenants and servants. Elizabeth Smith made it her business to know even the most intimate details about her tenants and their often complicated family connections with one another, causing some to take the view that she was an interfering 'busybody' and it is interesting that she once wrote:

> I am a very busy body, I think; the Colonel may laugh and I may sometimes fail, particularly where there are prejudices to fight against, still, some good must sometimes be done and every little helps.

After reading these extracts, readers can make their own judgements but it can hardly be denied that the story of the relationship between landlord and tenant in Ireland would have been very different if every Irish landlord had acted as humanely as did the Smiths of Baltiboys. Of course her own prejudices show. It must be kept in mind that a journal of the kind with which we are dealing is only one person's view of the life of a whole community, and in the case of Elizabeth Smith one who differed in religion, nationality and social class from the vast majority among whom she lived. It is probably fair to say that her occasional outbursts against the Irish, both of native and Anglo-Irish stock, are more informed by Victorian values of improvement and self-help than blind prejudice.

Although the Smiths were 'gentry' they were not especially wealthy and had, as already mentioned, inherited a very run-down property consisting of a relatively modest 1,200 acres, and valued at £1,200 a year in 1829. Elizabeth was, however, an efficient and prudent organiser and made the most of the limited resources that the family possessed. Lacking the wealth of some of the other local gentry, the Smiths did little of the socialising associated with that class and were content to cultivate their own small circle of friends.

While Elizabeth Smith gave different reasons at different times for keeping her journal, the principal one was, as she once wrote:

> for you, dear children, I am keeping this journal ... I have often during my life done so before, by starts ... and I have often regretted that I had not continued to do it .... My experience of life, my love for you, all make me anxious to devote myself to your welfare, and if it should be God's will to take your parents from you, the voice of your mother from the grave may be a guide and a protection. I am not young – and I am not strong.... Happiness, comfort, and care may lead us on yet many more years – but we may go sooner – before your principles are secured.

On another occasion, however, she stated that if the then current vogue for personal reminiscences continued, her journal might be published to provide her son Jack with a little additional income in later years. Little did she know that the reading public would have to wait a very long time before it could have that pleasure.

It must have taken considerable application to keep writing up the journal on a regular basis over such a long period and it is hardly surprising that, at times, Elizabeth's willpower wavered. Whenever this occurred her sense of duty was rallied by the need to set down her thoughts while they were still fresh in her mind. As she expressed it:

> If I intend this queer sort of journal of mine to be all interesting to us in our semidotage, when the fireside will be the better of the enlivening recollections of more active days. I had better write a little more regularly.

* * *

To set the scene, the decade of the 1830s, before she began her journal, was spent not only in her own house-building but in practical help to her tenants in order to improve their home and agricultural practices. She later described that time to her children:

> Your father's work and mine lay at home. We had work enough. We determined to get rid of all the little tenants and to increase the larger farms – and we did it – but not at once – just watched for opportunities and managed this delicate business without annoying anyone – or even causing a murmur. The departing were always furnished with the means of setting up in suitable employments, and were fully paid for any value left. We first repaired the thatch of all cabins – then put in windows – then built chimney stacks – not all at once either – little by little as people deserved help. Then your father built his house. The employment thus given completely set his tenants up – the pride they took in the place they had helped to make inspired them with a desire to improve their own dwellings, which was gratified by degrees as we could afford it. A better system of farming followed. The first field of turnips ever sown in these parts was what is now our front lawn. Then came the draining. The schools were set agoing. I remember that there was a great deal of trouble in the setting up the School – a sign of progress much wanted – none of the men and few of the women could read – none of the women could sew – method equally unknown in the home. Poor creatures they had been neglected for more than a generation.

And so, after nine years' work rehabilitating the estate, Elizabeth Smith began the task of writing her detailed Journal, noting down all that her observant eyes and ears saw and heard going on around her.

1840

"All thriving except old Shannon"

New Year's Day, 1840 was dark and rainy; Elizabeth Smith worked at the household accounts, paid all the debts and gave her elder daughter, Janie, a music lesson while her husband, Hal (whom she more often referred to as 'the Colonel') 'went out to look for the harriers and was the better for the ride'. In the evening the little family danced and, after the children had gone to bed, she read aloud part of *The Life of Wilberforce*. Recording ordinary, homely activities such as these, Elizabeth began her Irish journal. A few days later she was to give a first glimpse of a very different lifestyle, that of the tenants living in their tiny cottages on the Baltiboys estate:

> The little girls and I went to Widow Redmond's and to Biddy Shannon to send the children to school. How miserable was Shannon's cabin, the two families crowded together to save fuel, the asthmatick old man and his epileptick daughter, poor Biddy with five ragged girls, the three youngest infants – one at the breast, another hardly walking – God help them.

Readers of her journal also learn about the staffing of the house where there was:

> a cook, a housemaid who will wait on me, a nursery maid, Helen to come to do the washing and to be apart in her laundry as a day labourer – to finish it in four days – her wages 10/- [ten shillings] a month, finding her own tea, I feeding her, and every second Saturday to scrub the nurseries for which she will get her dinner. A butler and coachman completes our establishment indoors which a very little exertion on my part will keep in good order as they are a well disposed set of people.

Before the end of January, Elizabeth described the general state of the family and the reader gets a first glimpse of her outlook on life:

All of us in health. Children improving – dear Hal with plenty of the

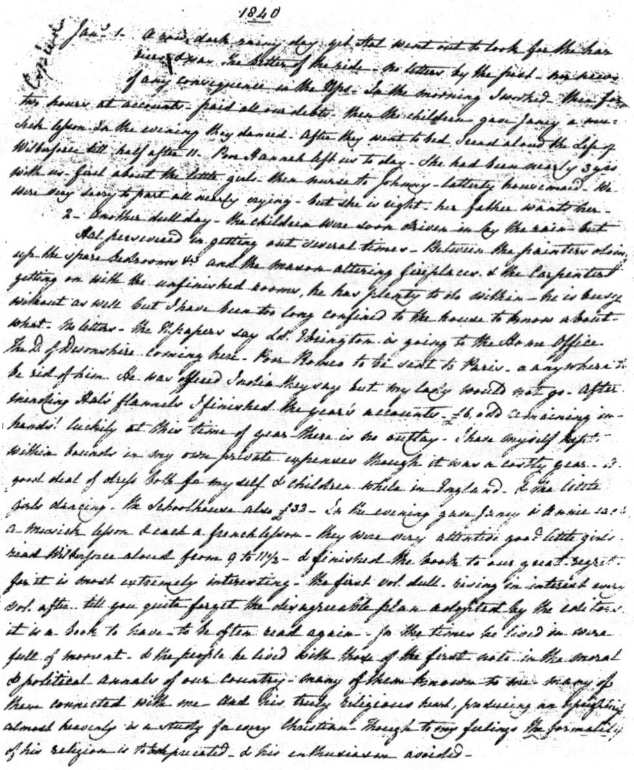
1840

Jany 1. A raw, dark, rainy day, yet Hal went out to look for the [illegible] [illegible] the bottom of the ride – no letters by the post – no news of any consequence in the [illegible] – In the morning I worked – then for two hours at accounts – paid all our debts – then the children gave Fanny a music lesson – In the evening they danced – After they went to bed I read aloud the Life of Wilberforce till half after 11 – Poor Hannah left us to day – She had been nearly 3 yrs with us – first about the little girls – then nurse to Johnny – latterly housemaid – We were very sorry to part all nearly crying – but she is right – her father wants her –

2 – Another dull day – the children were soon driven in by the rain – but Hal persevered in getting out several times – Between the painters doing up the spare bedrooms &c and the mason altering fireplaces & the Carpenters getting on with the unfinished rooms, he has plenty to do within – he is busy without as well but I have been too long confined to the house to know about what – No letters – the N. papers say Ld. Ebrington is going to the Home Office the D. of Devonshire coming here – Poor Robes to be sent to Paris – or anywhere to be rid of him – He was offered India they say but my lady would not go – After mending Hal's flannels I finished the year's accounts – £6. odd remaining in hands! luckily at this time of year there is no outlay – I have myself kept within bounds in my own private expenses though it was a costly year – a good deal of dress both for myself & children while in England – & the little girls dancing – the Schoolhouse also £33 – In the evening gave Fanny & Annie [illegible] a music lesson & each a french lesson – they were very attentive good little girls – read Wilberforce aloud from 9 to 11½ – & finished the book to our great regret – for it is most extremely interesting – the first vol. dull – rising in interest every vol. after – till you quite forget the disagreeable plan adopted by the editors – it is a book to have – to be often read again – for the times he lived in were full of moment – & the people he lived with those of the first note in the moral & political annals of our country – many of them known to me – many of them connected with me – And his truly religious heart, producing an [illegible] almost heavenly is a study for every Christian – though to my feelings the formality of his religion is to be deprecated – & his enthusiasm avoided –

The opening page of Elizabeth's journal, written on Wednesday, 1 January 1840, 'a raw, dark, rainy day'. (Patricia Pelly)

active business he likes on his own hands, and by good management, money enough to carry on his improvements gradually. Though far from rich, we are perfectly independent. We live comfortably – can afford to keep all about us – can see our friends in all hospitality – can give a little way – can assist many – and have the hope of bringing up the children – probably the happiest in our society – above want – below parade – leaving us at liberty to enjoy the quiet domestic life that suits us best. With a grateful heart do I acknowledge these blessings. May God Almighty keep me as I strive to be humble.

From time to time, Elizabeth gave different reasons for keeping her journal. First and foremost she saw it as a means of setting down standards for her children – especially in the event of her premature death. Twice during February she set the tone:

> Poor Widow Bankes came for some little presents. Do you remember, Janey and Annie, how frightened you were of this poor half crazy woman, and how Mama cured you by making her a sort of pet, giving you clothes for her, and letting you give her a dinner sometimes, little foolish girls, were you not?

Elizabeth's comments have a refreshing frankness, whether she was writing about the Queen, the government, Irish patriots, the clergy (of all denominations), the neighbouring gentry, the tenants or anyone else. Examples abound and here are just two written during the month of March, the first being about Lady Leeson of Russborough:

> Her Lord complaining that she never dresses till near dinner-time, an idle slovenly habit she learned in France, never stirs out, she that used to be so active, he don't know on earth what to do with her; so it must be she has no pursuit. With that beautiful house full of the choicest works of art she has no pleasure in it but to see it now and then dusted, her fine family of children are no resource to her. She is incapable of assisting in their education. No reader, beyond a novel which only wearies the spirits, no worker. And here let me remind you, dear little girls, of an old saying of dear Grandmama's that a woman who had not pleasure in her needle was never happy, and very seldom good, it may sound a little forced but it is nevertheless perfectly true ....
>
> Besides this want of occupation poor Lady Milltown has had the misfortune to yield to a vile, irritable, jealous, malicious temper which has alienated every friend, and of what avail to her is all her wit and her talent and her rank of which she is so vain now that she is getting old? The spirits that once carried her through are deserting her and she has nothing to replace them with, no one loves her, not even her children, I can't excuse her failings though I make every allowance for her entire want of education, her early marriage to a profligate man, her later marriage to an unprincipled one, for she *knows* the right way, and won't pursue it.

Baltiboys House was damaged during the 1798 rebellion and lay neglected for over 30 years until Elizabeth and her husband commenced the repairs. They did not always agree about how the work should be done and, as the following entry demonstrates, she was not averse to including criticism of Hal in her diary:

> Carpenters getting on well upstairs. Dear Hal mightily offended with me because I do not always approve of his taste. Like most men he

Baltiboys House, Elizabeth's Co. Wicklow home for more than 50 years, now almost surrounded by the waters of Pollaphuca reservoir. (Séamas Ó Maitiú)

> understands very little about colours, which contrast well, which suit, which shock, neither has he much eye for form or arrangement. Taste like every other talent requiring more cultivation than his active soldier's life has given him opportunity for, but I almost got myself into regular disgrace for hinting this. Men, you are very vain.

Another example of Elizabeth's frankness – and her astute powers of observation – occurred when she invited the Rector of Hollywood, the Rev. Mr Fetherstone, to bring a group of friends to Baltiboys:

> Wrote to Mr Fetherstone to ask him to tea. He came and the Doctor and two old Mr Murray's with two wives and six young people making a party of twenty-one. We had a long tea table, plenty of dancing, then wine and water and all seemed very happy. The Doctor was most good-natured doing all he could to keep up the fun, but the two curates declined dancing as too frivolous an act for the clerical profession and the two Carrolls on account of being in deep mourning, a mistake on the one part and folly on the other. What can be the sin of a clergyman standing up to dance with children in a small and perfectly private party, and when did young men ever introduce their feelings into society. Annoying a whole set of people for a piece of *self ceremony*, for they are quite able to laugh and eat most heartily, black crepe and all!

Baltiboys School was built by the Smiths before the re-building of their own house had been completed. It is now a youth hostel. (Séamas Ó Maitiú)

The Leesons of Russborough were close to the apex of the social pyramid in the social world in which Elizabeth now found herself. Joseph Leeson, son of a Dublin brewer, inherited his father's fortune and built his great house in the 1740s. It has been suggested that the name is a play on the Latin *rus in urbe.* The person who sold the site to Leeson was John Graydon whose family was related to the Smiths of Baltiboys, and Elizabeth's son Jack, was christened John Graydon Smith. The house is 700 feet long and built of granite from Golden Hill near Kilbride. Designed by the German architect Richard Cassells in the Palladian style, it consists of a central building flanked by two wings connected by semi-circular colonnades of alternate Doric and Corinthian pillars. The interior contains some of the best plasterwork in Ireland and also fine woodwork and mantelpieces. Russborough continued to be occupied by the Milltowns until the death, in 1890, of the sixth Earl. His bachelor brother did not inherit the estate which went instead to a nephew, Sir Thomas Turton, following whose death, in 1928, the property was sold to Captain Denis Daly. In 1952, Russborough was purchased by the late Sir Alfred Beit who then set about restoring the house and furnishing it with fine furniture and a world famous art collection. Sir Alfred established a charitable Trust in 1976 with the object of preserving intact the house and its contents which is open to the general public.

Joseph Leeson had become the Earl of Milltown in 1763, and in the 1840s the fourth Earl, also Joseph Leeson, lived at Russborough. He was a man of 41 years of age when we first meet him in the journal and in May 1840 Elizabeth wrote:

> In our drive this evening met Lord Milltown looking miserable – he said nothing of his winnings, and as his horses certainly lost, I fear he has made a bad business of it. What a life ..I never see him without a mixed feeling of sorrow and pity and shame that is really painful, for nature though she inflicted one very painful personal infirmity on him gifted him with many admirable qualities, fine talents, good understanding, amiable temper, very handsome countenance, and rank and wealth and zealous friends. A very bad education and an ill-sorted marriage have altogether made him to be shunned instead of courted, and he is himself most unhappy

References to his gambling crop up again and again when she speaks of Lord Milltown, and he turns out to be a compulsive gambler which, in those difficult times, brought him and his family close to disaster. His personal infirmity referred to is elaborated on later in the journal where he is likened to Mr Quilp in *The Old Curiosity Shop* who is described in Dickens' book as being 'so low in stature as to be quite a dwarf'. On another occasion she refers to Lord Milltown being wheeled into a room, so he probably was, for part of the time at least, in a wheelchair.

If she has feelings of sorrow and pity for the Lord her feelings for his wife, Barbara, Countess of Milltown, as we see above, are often of contempt and ridicule, although when the Smiths called upon her, as they often did, they were highly entertained by her gossip about the life of the well-connected and famous in Dublin and elsewhere.

* * *

Elizabeth walked quite a lot, sometimes alone or with one or more of the children. Frequently she mentions walking to and from Blessington (which she always spelt as *Blesinton*), a distance of just under two miles, or to Russborough, or around the estate visiting the tenants. It should be said here that the road to Blessington in the last century was shorter than the new road today because, prior to the building of the reservoir, the then more direct road traversed the now flooded land around Burgage church tower and graveyard.

In her first reference to walking to the village, she told how she went 'with the little girls' and called at Mrs Murray's. John Murray, her husband, was then the Agent of the very wealthy Marquis of Downshire who, besides owning considerable tracts of land in Counties Wicklow, Kildare and Kilkenny, owned even more property in County Down where he normally resided. The Downshire estate was unusual in that there was no big house attached. Lord Downshire's fine house overlooking the village was destroyed during the 1798 rebellion and was never re-built – indeed the ruins were removed about 30 years later. It is a matter of some curiosity that Elizabeth never commented upon where the Downshires stayed while residing at Blessington; it appears that they actually resided in the Estate Office in the village, now the Downshire Hotel.

The Hill family, ennobled as the Downshires, was one of the largest landowners in Ireland. The Downshires came into full possession of the Blessington estate at the end of the eighteenth century as a result of a marriage with the Boyle family, which had established the estate and town of Blessington.

Arthur Hill, the third Marquis of Downshire who regularly visited Blessington, was not liked by Elizabeth. When the Smiths first arrived in the neighbourhood they felt snubbed by him. Writing of him after his death she recalled: 'The late Lord never called upon me when I first came here although the Colonel waited upon him. The Colonel never went near him again'.

Her treatment of him in the journal is consequently unflattering. She describes him as having no attachments except to his purse. At half past eleven on the night of 17 April 1841, he arrived at the home of Mr Kilbee, inn-keeper and livery-stable owner in Blessington, only to find him in bed. His Lordship did not like being kept waiting. 'Hah, Mr Kilbee – in bed, hah, you go early to bed here Mr Kilbee'. 'People who pay so high for their land, my Lord, had need to be early in bed and early up.' Replied Mr Kilbee, without batting an eyelid.

Elizabeth considered Downshire to be weak, vain, pompous and self-important. His vanity comes through in an account of a conversation that is recorded in the same entry in the journal after it was reported to Elizabeth by a family friend and the local Blessington doctor, George Robinson. The Marquis whose estate, according to Elizabeth, earned him £7,000 a year, had given £10 to clothe the poor in Blessington. 'Mr Murray' he enquired of his agent, 'how is it, I gave £10 to the poor here a week ago and no mention of it in the newspapers, how was that?' His penny-pinching can be seen in a different light however when it is realised that by 1840 his family had incurred debts of £388,600 and the third Marquis made it an object of his life to liquidate these.

Landlords and near neighbours more in the Smith's own league were the Hornidge families of Tulfarris and Russelstown. The Hornidges were

Blessington Manor: The only known depiction of the seventeenth century Manor House built by Archbishop Boyle. Destroyed in 1798 it was never rebuilt. (Stan Hickey)

descended from a James Hornidge who had settled at Colemanna in County Carlow around 1656. Richard, his son was established at Tulfarris and Russeltown by 1700. Two sons of Richard, William and another Richard who lived at Russeltstown and Tulfarris respectively, gave rise to the two branches of the family we find in the 1840s. The opening year of the journal, marked the death of 'old John Hornidge', which is described by Elizabeth as a great loss to her husband, Henry who had served under him in the yeomanry in the rebellion of 1798. Other landed friends include the Cottons of Humphrystown, the Finnemores of Ballyward and the Henry family from Russelstown who were related to the Hornidges.

The meeting place for all these people was the little town of Blessington. In 1837 it had a population of 462 and in the early 1840s seems to have been a thriving place and, following a visit there, she described the scene:

> How that little village has improved since we first settled in this country eight years ago. And all since the market was established there, though John Hornidge, John Murray and other croakers declared it never would succeed and refused to encourage it. Colonel Smith, Ogle Moore and Doctor Robinson advanced the funds to set it agoing. Nothing more was required. Each week increased its business, by the end of the second year we were all repaid our advances. All the people round, better dressed, all busier, upwards of twenty new houses in Blesinton, most of them shops, each year the description of Shopkeepers and the style of goods improves. Those idle old men would keep a country back a generation.

An old viewof Blessington, which received a royal charter from Charles II in 1669. In the thirteenth century it was known as Villa Cumin. (PRONI)

This atmosphere of bustle and prosperity is reinforced by another visit she paid to the town:

> The evening being fine, we took a drive and found all the fashionable world in Blesinton – the village street being crowded with carriages. Mr Gilhooley's door and shop quite Grafton Street – the monthly fashions had arrived – the Miss Smith's muslin dresses had been finished according to the latest improvements and were there exhibiting to the publick.

At other times she mentions Mrs Merry the dressmaker, who made the Smiths' dresses, Gyves the nailer, Handsworth the grocer, Grace the butcher, (who made £5 profit per beast), Roberts the baker (careless to deal with), and Neale the tailor.

Apart from an occasional trip to Dublin, and even rarer visits to her mother and family in Edinburgh, Elizabeth seldom travelled very far and was always happy to get back to her beloved Baltiboys:

> Coming home, my heart filled thinking of all the happiness that waited us, business going forward everywhere, the ploughman in the field, the labourers splashing [slashing] the hedges, the farm yard full. It is really enjoying life to live as we do ... Hal and I walked all about to see what the men were doing, some fencing some potato planting. Beautiful weather, all prospering around us.

Elizabeth's first impressions of the tenantry were far from good. The well-being of these families and their ability to pay rents was important to the Smith estate. She recalled her first impressions in the journal:

> There stood to welcome me a crowd of as I thought, beggars – queer-looking men doffing the remnants of hats with much civility. 'Thim's the tenants', said the only man amongst them with a whole coat.

Perhaps there is a need to allow for at least some exaggeration here, as she would no doubt have wished to emphasise the low state of the tenantry when she arrived to contrast it with what she would have seen as their improved state, achieved through her own efforts, years later.

Elizabeth, as her readers soon discover, was interested in almost everything and her sharp eye missed very little; the household goings-on, the running of the estate, the lives of her tenants, the doings of the local gentry, the political and other news from elsewhere in Ireland, what the government in London – or even Queen Victoria – was up to, as well as the news of wars and rebellions abroad – almost everything that came to her notice seemed to be worth a comment.

One of the most effective means, she believed, of improving the tenantry and raising them from their debased state was through education. Even before the big house had been rebuilt she decided to start a school on the estate. There were a number of hedge-schools in the area of which she took a poor view. As early as 1834 she applied for recognition for her school in Baltiboys from the Board of Education.

The schoolhouse was converted by one of her tenants, James Ryan, at a cost of £80, which she paid him over three years. When the journal opens in 1840, a Miss Gardiner, whom the Smiths helped to train in Marlborough Street Model School, was employed. She taught about 25 small infants and older girls. The Smiths were highly pleased with her, and her work was praised by inspectors. When an inspector called in June 1841 the following pleasant scene was reported by Elizabeth:

> Thirty two children, very neat in their appearance ..the children answered well, they looked clean, happy and up to their business. The inspector was much pleased and said 'this is a very nice school, it is a pity it is so small'.

Despite the fact that Father Germaine, the parish priest of Black Ditches, now Valleymount, was a co-sponsor of the Baltiboys school, he tended to be suspicious of the religious intentions of the Smiths in relation to the childrens' education. The Smiths and the clergy of Black Ditches had a number of verbal clashes on this subject before a confrontation arose over a different matter. The Colonel had been nominated as a candidate for the Poor Law elections and was very annoyed when he heard that Father Germaine, had put forward a Mr Riley (Elizabeth's spelling) to oppose him. Further, Hal discovered that there had been:

> denunciations in the chapel against Colonel Smith and anyone who voted for him as a Poor Law guardian in opposition to the candidate of the true faith. He called on most of our tenants, threatened all, and rated all, yet all but two voted for their landlord. Dempsey stoutly insisted that he would, he did not care, he would vote for the man who gave him his land and he let the priest understand that it would be as well to give over abusing him for he was not the man who would bear it. The Curate struck him when Dempsey turned to the Priest, advised him to look after that young man of his for, as sure as he ever laid hands upon him again, so sure would he knock him down.

It is easy to understand the dilemma facing tenants caught between loyalty to their Church and their landlord. However, if Elizabeth had a poor opinion of the Roman Catholic church, she thought little better of the Presbyterians with whom she would have been very familiar in Scotland. On several occasions she referred to their 'morose character' and to their arrogance, sourness and bigotry. She also criticised the clergy of the Established Church with vigour and not a little sarcasm. She once described a sermon delivered by the Rector of Blessington as 'full of flourishes, splendid descriptions of flowery metaphorical language leading to nothing'. Indeed, bad sermons were the subject of Elizabeth's views on several occasion:

> Beautiful Sunday, full church, [St Mary's, Blessington] such a sermon, a whole chapter of Kings was the text, Ahab and Jezebel the subjects, connubial felicity the moral, in the unravelling of which he got into such a hobble that I let my veil down and sat quite in distress, there was no practical piety at all, a kind of lecture of folly.

St Mary's was built by Archbishop Boyle, who gave it a set of communion plate, an organ and a peal of bells which still bear the date 1682. The church has what is claimed to be the oldest public clock in Ireland.

In a journal entry about the local book society, of which she was a member, she wrote of the Reverend Ogle Moore, who was the Rector of Blessington and Kilbride, as well as the secretary of the society:

> We ought to have a new round of books ordered ... but our indolent secretary is too busy rocking his babies and fondling his wife to attend to any thing besides; how can we expect him to mind a book society when he neglects his parish?

It was this dereliction of their duties by some of the clergy that most often prompted Elizabeth's criticism:

> ... I could rake up fifty such cases or such like, where the total inattention of our clergy is every day increasing evils that a generation of better care will not eradicate. And people wonder that the reformed religion does not spread here. I wonder it is tolerated – it seems to fail to produce even in gentlemen an idea of their duty. What effect can it have on the poor. [The Rev.] Mr Moore is greatly more culpable than [the Rev.] Mr Foster – he knows his duty, which the other poor creature really does not – poor Ireland!

She sometimes saw all the churches in an equally poor light and once penned the following lines about the Anglicans, Roman Catholics and Presbyterians:

> ... how odious is priestcraft, how utterly opposed to the tenets of Him whom we pretend to consider is the author and the finisher of our faith. I really see very little difference between the Popish priest with his beads, his bells, and his vain repetitions, the Anglican Bishop with his purple and his palace and his retinue of humble expectants, and the arrogant Presbyter with his unyielding severity, assuming authority over laws and property, and praying with closed eyes against the sin of walking out in the fields on a Sunday.

After reading Whateley's *Errours of Romanism*, in which superstition and misdirected religious zeal were stated to be 'as rife among the members of the reformed church as ever it was among the papists' she added her own view that:

> ... to me, it has always appeared that we have changed *names* not *habits*. We are pagan idolaters still, have misunderstood the doctrines of our divine teacher, profaned His name, disobeyed His precepts and dishonoured the religion we pretend to.

This was the period of Father Mathew's (she spelled the name with two ts) crusade against drink and, when she was shown a temperance medal,

Elizabeth thought it 'rather handsome'. She was also impressed with the effects his remarkable campaign was having on the people:

> ... it is really curious what effect Father Matthew is producing, the distilleries are in many places given up, the breweries even injured. Our brewer told us he does not sell one cask of beer now for twenty he used to sell; that and the fine of five shillings really seems to have produced great effect; that odious whiskey, it is the bane of Ireland the money spent on this abominable poison would keep each family in comfort, besides that, with so excitable a people the use of spirits maddens them and puts them up to the commission of every crime ...

Later in the year, when Father Mathew was due to arrive at Black Ditches, as Valleymount parish was still called, Elizabeth was clearly impressed by all the reports of the success of his temperance campaign:

> Father Matthew to preach at Black Ditches to-day. Such crowds already on the road, the hill and the bridge swarming. All the country will be there; and no one before him ever did so much good to it, already rags are disappearing, the people are looking fat, clear, clean and more cheerful. In Blesinton, where I know every second house once sold whiskey, there are not above three in the whole town now where it is to be had. Coffee, tea and bread to be had in the teetotal shops instead, and on a market day quantities of meat bought. Drinking was the curse of the country, it is by no means so poverty stricken as it looked. The means of the people for the most part were fully adequate to their comfort, but they waste in riot what would have supported their families well. I have known a farmer take his oats to market and spend every shilling of the price of them in whiskey before he left it. Punch and a pipe – that was the Irish comfort, and to enjoy it he sat in a ruined cabin, in a ragged dress, by a cold hearth, with a starving set of children round him

* * *

In August, it was suggested to Elizabeth's husband that the family could actually save money by spending a couple of years abroad. Elizabeth warmed to the notion although two years were to pass before they implemented the idea. Perhaps it was the prospect of travelling to France that prompted Hal to draw up his will. As Elizabeth put it:

> Neither he nor I having any foolish superstitions about these things

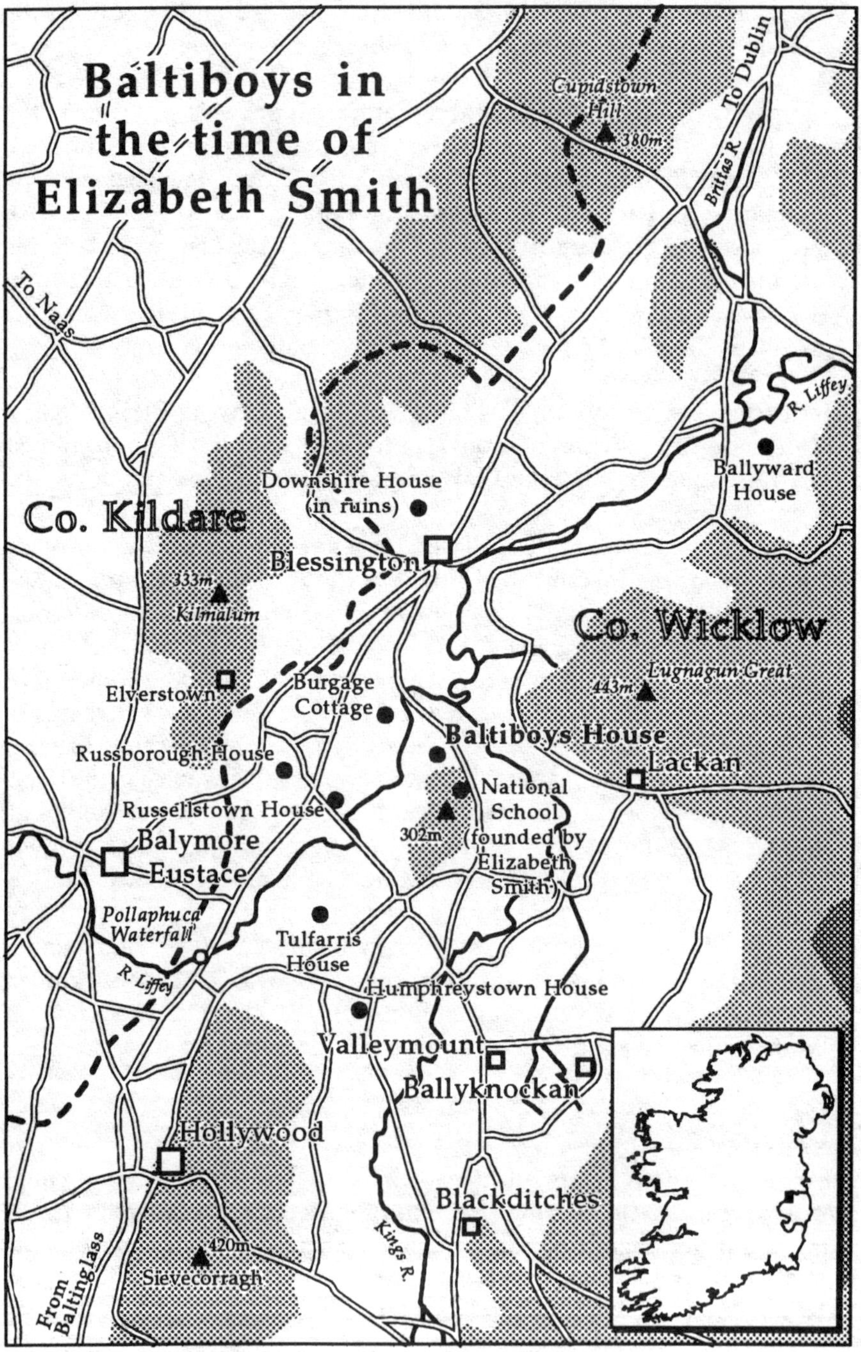

Matthew Stout

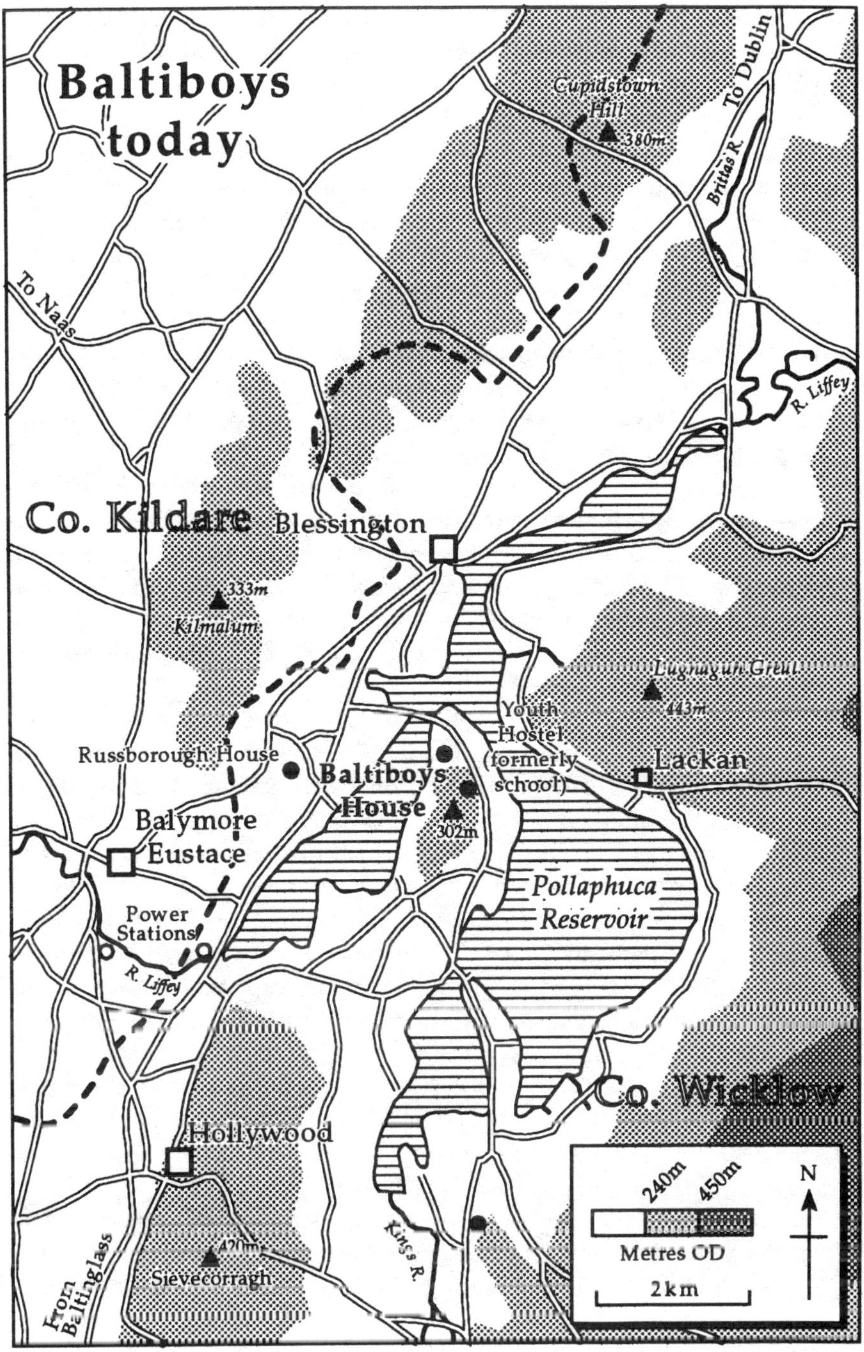

Matthew Stout

but both of us liking to have all our affairs so arranged that, in case of accident, all may be found in good order, properly settled, that there may be neither trouble nor perplexity left behind us.

Under the terms of this will he proposed to leave all his property to his son, then two years old, and £2,500 to each of his two daughters.

Thoughts of the possibility of going away also seemed to act as an incentive for Elizabeth to embark on a round of visits to check on the condition of all the tenants and, typically, she went on foot:

Took a long walk: went to school and was much pleased. Called in by Tom Kelly to see his new haggard. His whole range of offices is very complete, well laid out, well built and most creditable to him. He is in despair at the Colonel going away. So are they all, poor people. Old Mrs Tyrrell came to give up her land looking wretchedly ill. She has made some arrangement with Mick Tyrrell, which the Colonel seems to approve of, and which I hope may be agreed on, as the poor old woman would have her cabin and garden for life and a little turf, and be rid of her ill-tilled field, which keeps her in poverty and pays us no rent, and thus another patch would be got quit of, which fits in very well to little Tyrrell's good farm.

Began the round of visits I intend to make before leaving the Country, and took the Burgage side first. The Redmonds seem pretty comfortable; the eldest married daughter in a good place, paying the Mother for caring her fine child, and though receiving neither money nor kindness from her husband, able to maintain herself perfectly without him. The second daughter married too, rather in a hurry we think, and so well – to a woollen draper's shopman, quite a lift in the world – but when it happened and how she and her baby came so unexpectedly upon the scene, so immediately after the announcement of the husband, seems queer, however married she is and well, and has a comfortable lodging, and has taken her little sister Margaret to live with her. Biddy, too, is with a laundress, so only the two least girls are at home; tiny holdings. Mick always in work, and always dutiful to his Mother, so is her eldest son; her third son little help to her, but able to support himself, and she has a little boy as good as Mick. The house is in good repair, clean and decent, and she is so industrious there is no fear but that the worst days of that family are over. The poor Delanys looked miserable, their house a ruin and the two sick old people seated each side their chimney in patient misery. They have a little crop, straw enough to thatch the house, hay enough for the cow, the two little wee boys beginning to be some help to them, three daughters in good places, two at home – one

> must stay to mind those old cripples, but the other must get a place. Hal has left some warm clothing for the old man, and I must do something to enable them to get over the winter; it is heart-breaking to think of what will become of the creatures when we are away – it is the good dinner that has kept old Delany alive and free from pain so long. Then to the dear old cottage now almost a ruin, so dirty, so damp, windows overgrown with the creepers we trained so neatly, papers peeling off the walls, damp breaking through the ceilings, garden a wilderness. Mary Fitzpatrick wants what I can't give her – a contented temper – always fretting for evils she can't cure, and forgetting her many comforts. She would marry a Widower with three children, but only two of them are thrown upon her, and he is kind to her and a good workman. She has two nice babies of her own, wants nothing from me but a small supply of medicine, for her health is certainly very bad and most likely the principal cause of her fretfulness.
>
> We walked up Burgage Lane [four days later] to pay all remaining visits there, and found a great improvement in its inhabitants since we first remember them. All thriving except old Shannon, suffering from asthma, and Henry Wall's family, who don't look so well off as they used to do. The wife is too fond of tea; she has another baby, so I sent her physick. Mary Doolen I will leave a little money for, with Tom Darker, to be given to her occasionally.

When the rents became due at the end of November the tenants paid well with the exception of Pat Quin in the Bottoms 'who never will be anything made of', and Kearns:

> Little Doyle paid up all arrears, his fright having made him all industrious – that and the temperance pledge. Old Mrs Tyrrell has given up her holding to Mick Tyrrell, one of the most thriving farms in the place. Commins, as usual, had a mere nothing to give – three or four pounds and his tickets for butter.

Two days later the farm steward visited Commins to 'distrain' his goods and to make an inventory of the stock and crops, which were reckoned to be worth several hundred pounds. As a result, the agent produced for the Smiths 'two good milch cows, a yearling and some oats – altogether equal to the nine months rent owing. Why the old creature did not sell his things himself at the different fairs and markets and bring the money decently it would be hard to say'. Elizabeth was often baffled by what she saw as the duplicity of the tenants:

John [the agent] says that in the King's County when he is receiving Lady Milltown's rents, the tenants will pay a small proportion, fall on their knees, declare they cannot pay another penny, a thousand excuses from different pieces of ill-fortune; when he calls in the Driver, orders him to proceed immediately to distrain their goods, and then from out of some secret pocket comes the whole rent to a fraction. They are the strangest people! What has made them so it would be hard to tell: maybe misgovernment and certainly want of education and most indubitably the priesthood; but here they are, neither honest nor truthful nor industrious and full of wild fearful passions that won't be rooted out for many generations.

The poor Delaneys, who owe a dozen years rent, gave up their bit of ground at once and were forgiven their £15 or £16, which they were quite incapable of making in their best day, and now the old man's ill-health and the old woman's want of energy, for she is not so old or so weakly but what she could very well earn her bread, were it not for an indolent habit and the frightful doctrine that the more she suffers here, the less will she suffer hereafter. John got altogether upwards of £220. Rutherford and Williams have still to pay – another hundred nearly – and all the Bills we have in Dublin won't be quite a hundred, so that leaving me £60 for present expenses we will have a very nice little sum in hand, £150 I think, which we will not touch if we can help, that we may have a little ready money by us.

On Christmas Day, Elizabeth was unexpectedly reminded of Father Mathew's recent visit to the locality and she followed the entry with a brief note summing up the year:

What a pity – I forgot teetotalism when I mixed the puddings, and not one of the outside men would taste them. Now when those unruly people have such self-command, where they think it a sin to yield to temptation, is it not plain that properly educated they would be a fine and a moral race, almost equally plain that those thousand crimes they do commit they have not been taught to consider sins.

A regular reveillee – The Wren – under our windows. What can have been the origin of this strange custom? It is St Stephen's day – the first martyr, who was stoned to death – and what has a little harmless bird to do with that? They hound the poor little thing to death, then set it on a pole, fix a kind of bower round it, and then carry it all over the country with musick and dancing and all of them dressed up with all the rags and ribbons and bits of coloured paper they can collect. This morning there were no young women of the party as there used to be. Maybe they don't find it merry enough now that whiskey a'n't in fashion.

A visit from [the Rev.] Mr Moore and chatting on from one subject to another, he and I got quite confidential; he lamented his dereliction of duty, said he was firmly resolved to 'turn over a new leaf'. But you have said so often 'Never to you,' etc. He then went into some very painful family details, which did in some degree excuse his neglect of his parish duties, and appeared altogether so touched with the omissions of his proper business that I am in hope he will seriously set to work to repair them. And few could do it better, for his heart is kind, his temper gentle, his judgement good, his piety sincere and his manner delightful, yet I fear to trust him, he is indolent and facile, and unless his wife be impressed with the feeling of duty belonging to their station, I doubt his keeping his resolution.

* * *

Thus ends 1840. A year of quiet happiness spent entirely in our pleasant home, and in which, by prudence, we have managed to get before the world again. And all well. God be thanked for every mercy.

The Irish Times

Aerial view of Pollaphuca reservoir, photographed about 1953, looking north towards Blessington and Burgage with Baltiboys House in the foreground.

1841–42

"My whole heart is in Baltitboys"

The year 1841 saw a further gradual improvement in the state of Baltiboys and this applied to conditions for both the Smiths and most of their tenants. Early in the year Elizabeth Smith was to make an entry in her journal which would be almost meaningless to most people today: 'Sold all our lumpers at two pounds a ton, the produce of the old orchard, not an acre, value upwards of fourteen pounds ...' The Lumper was a variety of potato, widely regarded as very inferior in quality, taste and nourishment value, and often considered to be suitable only as animal fodder. The gentry and the better-off farmers grew the Lumpers for their livestock but the very poorest people grew them for their own consumption because they cropped heavily, a factor difficult to ignore by those who subsisted on the most marginal of holdings. Tragically, for the most vulnerable classes, this was the variety which proved most susceptible to the potato blight when it struck four years later.

Elizabeth's return of seven tons of Lumpers from less than one acre of an old orchard compares reasonably well with a national average potato yield of around six and a half tons to the acre. Much depended, of course, on the quality of the land and how well it was manured. The importance of applying manure to the potato drills was well understood even by the poorest people and a large, steaming dung-hill at the cottage door was something of a status symbol, even if Elizabeth disapproved of the proximity of the former to the latter. All appeared to be going well until, in the autumn, Elizabeth wrote:

> Such a season, God help us for I am sure man can't, potato crop a failure, corn malting [sprouting] in the stooks, no fuel, misery ... our potatoes are too bad to keep over the winter, they were very dear as was all stock this year.
>
> What will become of the improvident poor of this country, in the Poor House some must be driven to take refuge, but it won't contain a fourth part of the starving population and many of them will die rather

than enter it and many, many a decent family will suffer bitterly and won't complain. It is all very well for such as we are. We may get less rent and be obliged to forego some luxuries, some pleasures, but necessaries we can always command in plenty, the most evil to us would be to have to give up a workman or two and so to throw industrious creatures out of bread, it is all very miserable.

In the course of these few sentences, Elizabeth made a series of acute observations and actually foresaw some of the serious consequences of the famine that was to come in 1845:

- The over-dependence of the poor upon the potato crop.
- Starving tenants would be unable to pay rent, posing serious consequences for the landlords.
- The landlords would not starve but their standard of living would drop significantly.
- The landlords would dispense with expendable workers who would then join those already starving.

Sooner or later the over-dependence on potatoes was going to have disastrous consequences. Even if the blight had never arrived, it was inevitable that the potato crop sometimes failed as had just happened in 1841. The actual numbers so dependant probably exceeded two million people and the danger was greatly compounded by the fact that almost all of them had no option but to grow their tubers on the same small plots year after year. Such a system, monoculture, resulted in a build-up of diseases and was a recipe for disaster. Given that about fifteen million tons of potatoes were grown annually at this time, and that the average personal consumption was about six or seven tons, nothing short of a massive re-distribution of land could have averted a calamity.

The 1841 potato crop set-back recorded by Elizabeth mirrored similar partial crop failures including those of 1816 and 1821 and, in addition, several forms of blight or disease had also struck. The first of these came as early as the middle of the eighteenth century and was known as 'the curl'. A more serious blight appeared in Ireland about a dozen years before the Famine and was called 'the taint', or 'dry rot'.

However, the effects of the 1841 potato shortage were not as serious as was first thought and this appears to be confirmed by a journal entry at the end of November after John Robinson, the Baltiboys agent, collected the half-year rents:

John made us quite happy in the evening by his account of the tenants;

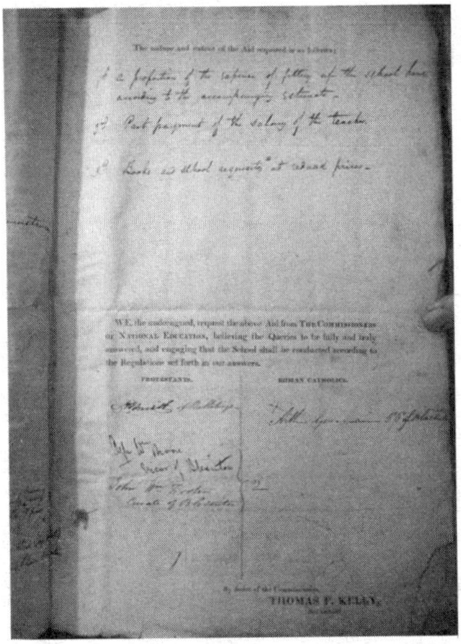

WE, the undersigned, request the above Aid from THE COMMISSIONERS OF NATIONAL EDUCATION, believing the Queries to be fully and truly answered, and engaging that the School shall be conducted according to the Regulations set forth in our answers.

PROTESTANTS. ROMAN CATHOLICS.

THOMAS F. KELLY,

Application to the Commissioners of National Education seeking assistance in setting up the school in Baltiboys. The signatures include that of Elizabeth Smith.

> trying to farmers as the season has been – with the untoward weather and mortality among the cattle – they have paid well, are all forwarder than they were this time last year and so decently dressed, clean, whole, comfortable looking, many of them with good cloth body coats and all good frieze coats, very different indeed from the ragged crew that welcomed me to Baltiboys just ten years ago this past October. It makes one feel very happy to see such improvement year by year among old and young, it is worth some personal sacrifice if indeed it can be called sacrifice to substitute the substantial pleasures resulting from properly fulfilled duties for mere selfish gratifications.

The engagement of an agent is indicative of the business-like way landlords attempted to deal with their tenants. Robinson came on gale-days from his office in Talbot Street, Dublin to collect the rents, from which he obtained a percentage. He also acted as agent to the Milltowns and combined his agency business with his main activity as a corn factor. From small beginnings his business affairs grew to the point where, according to Elizabeth, he earned £12,000 in 1845. The Smiths, whose income at the time was about a tenth of this sum, would regularly borrow money from him against the rent.

* * *

Paupers, as Elizabeth often noted in her journal, lived in terror of being sent to the Poor House though, judging from her descriptions of the conditions under which the inmates lived, this was hardly surprising. People often called to Baltiboys House seeking help and if one can come to a conclusion from reading her own reactions, they seldom went away empty-handed:

> A poor old body came to get help to stock a basket so I fitted it up in a way. Hal says that they have a notion that if they even have the merest shadow of trade they will not be sent to the poor house, this trade then will not keep this poor body long out of it.

Her descriptions of her various servants and what they got up to often make for delightful and sometimes amusing reading:

> Really quite tormented with little Caroline, she has taken quite a mania for dress and she clips and works at the bodies of her gowns till she can hardly stuff herself into them and patches on great bits at the bottom till her petticoats trail all round upon the ground and, after her tour with Johnny on wet days, she comes in with a quarter of a yard of mud about her legs; her bonnets too, she won't wear unless they are of the fashionable shape and she is such a plain little thing, she can only look well by being, very clean and very neat.

Elizabeth's efforts to obtain a kitchen maid for her friends, the Finnamores of Ballyward, met with a degree of difficulty the cause of which was, she explained:

> ... the progress of civilisation, indisposing any girl who has a hope of doing better to take a situation where the women servants sleep on a shakedown in the *kitchen*, three together, bring all the water from the river, wash all the potatoes for man and beast, have low wages, meat but twice a week cut into portions in the parlour and sent out in portions. They would bear this well in a farmer's house and be glad to get the place, but when with this low degree in kitchen, there is the utmost profusion in hall with great finery at times and grandeur of position, always they who practise such contradictions must be content with the refuse of the servant class ...

After writing about the diverse number of tasks which she was either doing, contemplating or supervising, she noted in her journal:

> I am a very busy body I think, the Colonel may laugh and I may sometimes fail – particularly where there are prejudices to fight against, still some good must sometimes be done and every little helps.

During the last weeks of 1841 and into the new year of 1842, Elizabeth had not been feeling well. In fact, she was suffering from a 'phantom' pregnancy which explains the following curious entry:

> No use in writing daily in this stupid journal. It is a plague to get at my writing materials and the position is awkward and my brains a'int always clear, and very little is going on. Hal hunting, children well, me myself but indifferent, well enough in health but always something going wrong with the baby – it will be a little wonder if it survives all its misfortunes...

Elizabeth's *Journal*, at this time, tended to focus either on the news from abroad or the minor goings-on around her:

> Lady Milltown and her five children to tea; the Doctor dropped in at eight so we had whist in one room, romping in the other – plenty of laughing in both – for that is a most amusing woman, full of wit, full of fun, full of scandal, and not particular as to accuracy, her tongue never stopt for one moment; we played our cards certainly, but as for playing the game that was not possible. Story after story – jest after jest – husband – kindred- acquaintance – all served up with sauce *piquante* for our entertainment.

Elizabeth's frankness in her comments about people and, indeed about herself, has been noted before. At the beginning of June she began to have some doubts about the wisdom of committing such forthright opinions to paper:

> I have been thinking whether it has been quite right in me to set down for evil as well as for good in this written exposure of feelings which I intend to be read by my children, all my private opinions of people and people's actions, some of them very near and very dear to me. My tongue I know often goes too fast, my pen too, I suppose, for it runs on over the words just as the tongue does. However, dear children, you may just remember this that whether what I feel be wrong or right it is my honest impression at the time.

In June, Archdeacon Agar and his wife, who lived near Hollywood, called to Baltiboys after a long absence. They were obviously a little odd, and apparently not very good at managing their affairs or keeping up appearances but, for all that, they were very much liked by Elizabeth:

> Their strange old gigs and chaises and phaetons [carriages], the nondescript harness and elderly horses were quite missed on the roads; and the pair themselves, I missed them too – her comely, *sonsy* [plump] face and figure, his clever, odd, amusing conversation and perfectly gentlemanly manner. The Archdeacon don't get tipsy by himself but he drinks plenty and variety and the best, and for eating – *loads* of the best and richest and rarest – half cooked by himself – wholly served – for they seem to have but one bare[footed] maid and Mrs Agar's own attendant.
>
> When people call, the Archdeacon takes their horses to the stable having no man to do it. When Mr Fetherstone slept there, the Archdeacon carried up his shaving water, took away his dirty boots; there was no one else to do it. In the tiny glebe house there are neither carpets nor curtains. On a side table are generally to be seen the half burned pair of tallow candles of the night before, the butter left from breakfast, a regular row of black bottles, full and empty. She seems to do little but patch her old gowns with a placid smile that never varies. Both are odd – decidedly – his family cleverly odd – hers foolishly ditto. Their wealth between them, for each brought with them a goodly portion to the joint stock, would be great for anyone – to them with their habits it is boundless; the strange thing too is that he with a mind so full of ideas should be content with her society and that she without an idea and brought up in the busy frivolity of London life can content herself with solitude. They seem perfectly happy – on the most agreeable terms – satisfied – both of them.

Elizabeth continued her regular visits to the tenants and from her descriptions of them can be seen how remarkably well she knew them all, their strengths as well as their weaknesses, their often complicated relationships with each other in a tight-knit community. If her observations were sharp, and if she was firm with those who made no effort to improve themselves, she nevertheless comes across as a genuinely caring and compassionate person. One of the tenants who was the cause of some concern was Judy Ryan, a woman described by Elizabeth as being capable of 'dishonesty, trickery and attempted cuteness', whom the Smiths persuaded to vacate her holding:

> ... poor Judy, she gives up her grounds this day, taking her goods and

> her youngest child with her; the goods I believe will not much burden her, every day decreasing the load. Stock she has never had. Hal gives her £10 to go off peaceably, £5 for her child, Jane her eldest girl is to be added to *my* family; the boy he takes himself and intends putting him apprentice to a good trade. So poor Christy Ryan's children, orphan children, have not been neglected by their Landlord.

On the following day, Elizabeth described how Judy Ryan called to the house:

> to get a little money to purchase clothes for her *wedding*, having announced her approaching marriage to *John Doyle* in the Bottoms, an ill-tempered queer looking skeleton with some ten or twelve acres of ground who wants some thatch on his house, some stock on his land etc. They may do pretty well for he is industrious, but it is strange to me that she would not rather remain independent.

Judy Ryan's marriage, her second, took place just over two weeks later after which Elizabeth was told that the parish priest: 'hearing she had been well paid for giving up her land insisted on £2 for marrying her. She resisted, paid but £1, battled the point with him and complains loudly of his extortion. Changed times'.

Tom Kelly, another tenant, but with eighty acres, lived in better circumstances even if he 'wallowed in dirt' and was generally untidy. When Elizabeth called after a long absence she was received 'with rapture':

> They are models of the comfortable small Irish farmer – rich with their eighty acres of tolerably managed land, wallowing in dirt and plenty. Such thorough untidiness. Beautiful butter, three large cools worth at least £4 kept in the bedroom; the children sleeping on straw laid on chairs, mahogany table inch thick with dirt, disorder all round, but good new offices, fine cattle, splendid cabbage, with pease, beans and turnips in a garden, door half destroyed by surface water accumulating in consequence of the drain being choked; the garden door too, was off its hinges, so it was the more easily laid over a gutter full of filth through which it would hardly have been agreeable for us to wade. Tom pulled us all by the sleeve here and there to see his different improvements, apologising in the old way for the old deformities.

Elizabeth did not assume that her regular rounds to the tenants would invariably produce positive results. 'Our visits may not do much good but they can do us no harm so I will continue with them as usual though I

Pat Quin of the Bottoms lived in this house which survived substantially unaltered until 1939 when it was demolished by the ESB, and his descendants still living there were moved elsewhere. More than 70 homes were acquired by compulsory purchase orders and, even though compensation settlements were made, some of those affected regarded their resettlement as little better than eviction. The story is still told locally that a neighbour of the Quins' remained in his house until the floodwaters entered his home and he had to be taken away by boat. (Dept. of Irish Studies, UCD.)

don't set them all down here, only when they suggest reflections to me.'

* * *

During the month of August 1842, Elizabeth described the daily routine in her household thus:

> Another beautiful day, plenty to do but little to record; it would be one eternal history of domestick economy were I to set down regularly the details of our peaceful lives ... The usual routine – business in the morning, a little walk, a little reading, a drive, another walk, and the day is over.
>
> Last night we called upon John Young and his wife ... who have four children at school. A very talking woman, very conceited, very ignorant, but very nice looking, perfectly tidy in her person and with the cleanest house I ever set my foot in here-abouts. She is not satisfied quite with Miss Gardener's mode of teaching. She understands she never thumps the pupils and they never will learn unless the master be severe on them. She now and then sends her directions what they are to be taught and how, and to have them kept well to their tasks, no play – what does she pay for and slave for, etc.? What a mine of patience it

requires to deal with the ignorant.

A romantic view of the pre-famine Irish countryside might incline one to the view that, apart from agrarian outrages, it was a relatively crime-free place. This appears to have been far from the reality. A number of thefts are recorded in the journal. The poultry-house of an elderly tenant, Peggy Dobson, had been commented on as been broken into in November 1841 and four fat turkeys, which she had been fattening for Christmas, stolen, causing her great distress. Indeed poor Peggy seems to have been a soft target for thieves, because some years later, she was robbed of her best clothes – a new cloak, two good gowns, blankets, sheets and some money. A man and woman, of what Elizabeth calls, 'pedlar appearance' were suspected, and although they were supposed to have been seen near Naas, could not be traced.

A misdemeanour of a sexual nature was recorded by Elizabeth in the journal in November 1842; the topic is introduced in enigmatic fashion:

> Wretched day, not cold however. The Dumbie was to go to Naas to the workhouse, herself and her unhappy baby, whose cries she can't hear and whom she has no means of providing for.

This deaf and dumb woman had been living among the neighbours all her life earning her food and clothing by hard labour and the charity of rich and poor alike. She had been working for a local farming family about two weeks before this reference in the journal bringing in baskets of potatoes from the field when she was suddenly missed. She was found in a cow-house with a new-born infant. The wife of the farmer for whom she was working brought her into a hay loft and gave her some gruel. When the deaf and dumb woman by sign language accused the brother of the farmer's wife, a man of the surname Butler, for causing her situation she was turned out on the road, almost naked, but for a few rags, her baby wrapped in an apron.

She lay 'in the gripe of a ditch' all day until taken in by Dick Gray, 'almost the poorest man in Baltiboys'. It transpired that the guilty man slept in the hay loft as the only companion of the deaf and dumb woman. Elizabeth claimed that the Colonel did all in his power to make the family pay for their unchristian conduct, but the law could not help. She also claimed the clergy in Black Ditches believed the woman's story who, in their register, gave the little girl the name Butler. A search in the baptismal register of what is now Valleymount parish failed to locate the appropriate entry, but there are a number of pages missing for these years. A tradition in the parish has it that the unfortunate woman later emigrated and died in the great fire in Chicago in 1871.

Improvements to Baltiboys House were continuing and those already made were beginning to show to good effect. James Frazer, whom Elizabeth termed 'the *capability* man', arrived and went for a very long walk around the estate with the Colonel. It was Frazer, apparently, who had advised the Smiths on some of the improvements – hence Elizabeth's use of the term *capability*, after the famous landscaper, Capability Brown (1715-83). Frazer had returned to see how some of his suggested improvements had worked out:

> He was surprised at the beauty of the place which he had formerly seen to great disadvantage in bad rainy weather at an ungenial season. This day the whole country looked well; the planting everywhere has grown too and the new approach [drive] and other alterations, some of them suggested by himself, have all been well carried out and greatly improve the appearance of the place. The fields above the house enchanted him – the lay of the land is so particularly pretty and the views everywhere are so fine – he says it will be a lion some day – a place to come to see.
>
> I have no good eye myself for laying out grounds though I can beautify them well enough when the general effect is arranged for me; but I quite understand the pleasure there must be in the capability on designing on this large scale and can feel the full beauty of embellished scenery. And the interest of the works while going on no one can enter into more completely. My whole heart is in Baltiboys – our dear happy family – the pretty place – the people – the last the least improvable.

* * *

There was a very severe thunderstorm during the same month, which served to remind Elizabeth about a different kind of storm which she herself had unwittingly initiated, and which caused her to reflect upon her dealings with other people. The incident began innocently enough when she and her husband were out walking around the estate and came across some women weeding the Colonel's turnips. Elizabeth called out to one of the women: 'Why Mary, you'll be a year at that work; look here, have you no hoe?' She then stepped into the field to give a demonstration on how to use a hoe after which she volunteered to go back to the garden to fetch one. As she turned to go, she was, as she expressed it:

> amazed at the check given by the Colonel's strange coolness to my

> precipitancy. Not without reason did Hal look grave – I had never thought about Tom Darker.

Darker, the Colonel's steward, verbally attacked his employer the next day, after he had heard about the incident, regarding it as an interference in his duties. The Colonel had some difficulty in calming him down, reassuring him how much his work was valued, adding that it was simply not true to say he was regarded as other than a first class farmer. A somewhat chastened Elizabeth then recorded.

> It comes out that *Scotch* methods, *Scotch* tools, *Scotch* books, and alas! the *Scotch* mistress, were the aggravating causes of all this absurdity, producing the Irish jealous fear that I wanted to get rid of him to give his place to a *Scotchman*. This is my reward for devoting time, thoughts, money – more than I can spare – to the improvement – moral, social and intellectual – of this strange land wherein my lot late in life has been cast ....
>
> Tom Darker is not alone in his unkind feelings to a foreigner. Many a rub, many a scowl, many an insolence has the *Scotch Lady of Baltiboys* had to bear from those depending on her for their bread .... It is a good lesson in more ways than one. I had fancied myself grown very cautious in my manner of hinting – avoiding all collision with prejudice, or any hasty stride toward better ways – probably I have been teasing poor Tom and others with my farming books and cottage economy and value of time.

Elizabeth's affection for her Irish home is a recurring theme. She was to repeat it while on a visit to her mother in Edinburgh: 'Dear Baltiboys ... I am longing for the country, our green fields, our woods, our river, my gardens and all my home occupations...' During another stay with her Scottish relations, she expressed similar sentiments about Ireland: The Scots, she said:

> ... certainly don't show to advantage after Ireland. I have no wish to change my quarters, but there are many admirable people here, much to admire, much to copy, and were it necessary, I could live very happily in Edinburgh *for a season.*

On the other hand, some months later she commented on how the Scots and the Irish differed in the matter of disputes:

> Would that such [Scottish] calmness could reach Ireland, where the violence of every feeling is displayed with the heat and the folly of

> lunaticks. All sides sinning alike, all parties, all creeds, and on all matters, publick, scientifick, religious and domestic. They will fight to frenzy about the placing of Jack straws.

After her return to County Wicklow, Elizabeth remarked upon the fact that her absence had resulted in her journal being neglected:

> Here ends October and if I intend this queer sort of journal of mine to be at all interesting to us in our semidotage, when the fireplace will be the better of enlivening recollections of more active days, I had better write a little more regularly in it than I have done of late, and more particularly for at present full half of the impressions it would be as well to remember escape altogether any notice, and the remainder get but small justice.

* * *

Ending her 1842 journal on 31 December, Elizabeth reflected:

> I am writing on, and somehow I don't like parting with the old year ... it is never a merry farewell, do what we will with it, for alas, as years run their course they seem to get shorter and shorter, leaving, in spite of our best intentions, too many things undone.

1843–44

"Twelve busy years have we lived here"

Early in January, Elizabeth Smith described the country as 'looking well, the people in spirits, and here at least we know nothing of the turbulent opposition to the Poor Laws which is distracting the south'. The latter was her first reference to a subject which was to surface many times later – including this one at the end of the same month:

> Meetings everywhere about some alteration in our Irish Poor Laws; it is becoming more unpopular every day and is a subject altogether beyond my comprehension. This plan seems to do little good and to cost much – no one proposes a better – misery is encreasing. All an individual can do is to employ as many workmen as possible, and give as much spinning, knitting and needlework, in short any work that can be done at home and as they can afford, to the women.

The Smiths continued in their efforts to improve the Baltiboys estate and to complete the repairs to their own house but they were still hampered in their efforts because of insufficient finance:

> The estimate for completely finishing the house inside and outside will be, in round numbers, at the most £150, but this without chimney pieces, grates, or paper in the two lower rooms or fine painting the wood in the drawing room. We have made out that we ought to get £200 for what we have to sell, which will leave a balance the right way.

Several years earlier it had been suggested to them that they could not only save but should actually accumulate money by going abroad for a year or two, renting Baltiboys House and some of the land. Elizabeth's aunt, Mary Bourne, wrote in April to again advise the Smiths to go to France:

> She is very anxious about me, speaks most sensibly about the wisdom

of taking things in time; argues so very justly about the numerous advantages of a change to all of us that I believe she will prevail. Much as both of us love this place, sorely as we regret living away from it, there are many reasons which make the plan desirable. Hal has made up his mind to it, I think, and I believe all he *well* considers he always decides rightly on. My kind Aunt then proceeds to say that though she gives a good deal of her income away, as I know, she yet saves a good deal, and that fearing my Mother would be slenderly provided for in the case of my father's death, she had made her will leaving the interest of all her little savings to my Mother for her life: at her death small legacies among us, and *me* her residuary legatee. Thus between the portion my father is to leave me and what my kind Aunt has willed me, dear Hal will get sufficient to provide for his two little daughters without encumbering poor Jack's inheritance.

In May 1843, they made up their minds to go to France for two years and Elizabeth documented the early plans for the family's departure:

Having determined on going abroad for two years we have offered to let this house for that term, furnished, with the garden, orchard and good stabling and for a good tenant might throw a cow's grass into the bargain, asking £150 a year and the gardener's wages. It is a good house for a private gentleman even in its unfinished state ... We shall sell the Jaunting car, all the harness and saddlery, all the riding horses. We hope that the sale of all these will pay our journey to Pau, and that the rent of the house with the Colonel's pay will be sufficient to keep us there. Then we can leave the rents of the Irish property to accumulate, as Tom Darker thinks the profits of the farm should nearly pay all the unavoidable expenses attending the estate.

... We all feel the parting, indeed the break up altogether is far from pleasing. We were so happy here, were doing so much good, all was thriving round. Twelve busy years have we lived here in the enjoyment of all that could make rational beings comfortable ...

The darker side of all this was the unsettled political situation which Elizabeth blamed on the 'Repeal absurdity which sooner or later will come to bloodshed', another good reason, she thought, for the family to make preparations for their proposed departure to France. 'No one need wish to stay in this country till it be a little safer to live in it'.

The forties saw the last eight years of the man who, without resorting to violence, probably achieved more for Ireland than anyone else before or since. Daniel O'Connell, having already secured Catholic Emancipation began to employ similar methods, using his already powerful movement of mass support, to embark upon the Repeal of the Act of Union. His aim was to secure, once again, an independent parliament in Dublin which, however, would be different in composition from that abolished in 1801. The new legislature, if he could secure it, would not be dominated by the Ascendancy but by the newly emerging Catholic vote. Elizabeth's dismissive remark about the Repeal movement as 'the Repeal absurdity' reflected the view of most of her class. She had no great opinion of the movement's charismatic leader either, she once called O'Connell 'a patriot a little mad' and in her very first reference to him, in January 1840, she wrote that he was 'telling unblushing falsehoods as usual and using language in the House [of Commons] such as he uses to his mobs ...' On one of her visits, Lady Milltown told Elizabeth that 'Mr O'Connell has been merely making tools of the patriots to fill his own purse', repeating rumours readily believed by those who preferred the status quo, that very large sums of collected money were not accounted for.

When, in May 1842, Daniel O'Connell addressed a huge meeting at the Curragh, it is clear that the Smiths did not approve of their tenants lending support to the Repeal cause either:

> The only one of our tenants who attended [there] ... was Pat Ryan. I am inclined to hope it was only curiosity that took him there but it was a very foolish proceeding and will prevent the Colonel adding to his farm as he intended ...

A month later, returning home to Baltiboys along Featherbed Lane, the Smiths came across a large crowd

> ... at least 150 people who had been all to see O'Connell pass; he had changed horses at Mr Kilbee's [in Blessington] on the way to Baltinglas where he performs tomorrow. Blesinton was filled with a mob of the unwashed, but there was no enthusiasm among them, we heard – mere curiosity for the most part.

One of Elizabeth's friends, Anne Henry, who lived across the river at Russellstown, told her in June 1843 that:

> O'Connell is in great fright, pushed into measures he never contemplated, he has raised a flame he cannot quench, they would turn on him and destroy him if he were now to recede.

When Colonel Smith returned a bond to one of the tenants and, in the process, 'lightened the man's load', Elizabeth was told: 'Faix! were they all sich landlords as the Colonel, Mr O'Connell might go whistle for repalers'.

* * *

On 8 August 1843, the Smiths left Baltiboys for France, where they stayed for one year at Pau, followed by a second year at Avranches, returning to Ireland in July 1845.

1845

"Two damaged potatoes, the first we have seen"

After her return from France, Elizabeth Smith noted that there was an additional £430 in the bank: probably in excess of £25,000 in today's money, and she cheerfully noted down that 'we have not been so rich for many years'.

Settling back in Baltiboys, Elizabeth continued her life much as before, finding her 'humbler neighbours' all thriving, 'a great change for the better since I last made my rounds among them'. She commented upon the 'rainy weather, very rainy', annoyed because of its effect upon the almost ready-to-harvest hay and also because it interfered with her walks. What she did not realise, nor did anyone else, was that the wet summer of 1845 was to be a significant factor in the spread of the potato blight which was to manifest itself only a few weeks later.

The blight had occurred in the United States two years earlier and had spread to Europe in June, 1845 where it was first noticed in Flanders. Weather records show that western Europe generally had an overcast, cold and wet summer – ideal conditions, as is now well known, for the spread of the disease. The blight was caused by the fungus, *Phytophtora infestens*, which rapidly spread northwards to Scandinavia, eastwards to Prussia and Poland, south to Spain and even to north Africa, and westwards to Britain and Ireland. Fungal diseases were not understood at the time and the only known (partial) remedy was the need to introduce new potato strains and it may be a sad irony that new, infested potatoes may have been the means of carrying the disease to Europe.

The first reference to the disease in Elizabeth's journal was written on 26 October 1845:

> The month of October is running rapidly away, the weeks actually flying. The Colonel has been very much occupied with plans for the prevention of such extreme distress as the failure of the potato crop threatens the poor with. Just in Baltiboys there seems as yet to be no damage done but very near at hand this widespread disease has already

Russborough, the fine mansion of the Leeson family, Earls of Milltown. Elizabeth, a regular visitor, once described it as 'that cathedral of a house'. (Séamas Ó Maitiú)

Detail from the old Market House in Blessington, showing the coat of arms of the Marquis of Downshire. (Séamas Ó Maitiú)

attacked some large con-acre fields where the poor man's supply for the next nine months may, without active measures speedily taken, fail him entirely. The potato once attacked is quite unfit for food, it rots away, infecting all its companions, but the farina, the nourishing part of the root, is uninjured even in the worst cases so that by scraping down the potato at once and making it into what they call starch nothing fit for food is lost. This starch or flour mixed with a half of wheaten flour makes delicious bread some of which we tasted to-day for Mr Shehan amongst others has been trying this experiment and he sent us by young John Hornidge a sample. Corn is an abundant crop, and though rising in the market at present during this panick it is expected shortly to fall, particularly if they open the ports to foreign corn free of duty which we hear the Government will do if necessary ....

Hal fears the want of energy of the lower orders, their idleness, and their ignorance will prevent their setting to work to supply themselves with this change of food so he went to see Mr Owen on the subject of establishing a scraping manufactory and perhaps a bakery, and he found him quite ready to do everything to lessen this calamity.

Up to the beginning of November, Baltiboys had escaped the ravages of the blight which seemed to be all around but, on 4 November, Hal brought in 'two damaged potatoes, the first we have seen of our own, for on our hill few have been found as yet'. Six days later the Baltiboys steward expressed concern about their second potato field. 'The first had hardly a bad potato so that he was unprepared for this.' A few days after this the journal recorded that 'half of the potatoes of this new field are tainted, some very badly'.

Elizabeth's husband attended a meeting to consider 'fit measures for the relief of impending evils on account of the potato famine disease'. After remarking how nearly impossible it was 'to manage the ignorant except by force, gentle force if practicable', she wrote about her despair of their tenants' inability to help themselves:

Some of the dull old people hereabouts decline making starch of their bad potatoes, it can't be wholesome, if the potato be tainted the starch must be tainted and so unfit for food. We have explained to many the structure of the root and how the farina escapes when the fibrous part suffers, and wonderfully well some of them understand, by the help of the illustration of the honeycomb, others are quite obtuse and mean to sit down with folded hands to bear the Will of God, in other words relief from the benevolent without any exertion on their part.

She commented that there were only two families in real distress in Baltiboys at that time:

> George Kearns [she sometimes spelt the name 'Cairns'] who will soon by his own activity be out of it, and John Byrne, uncle to Jack, and an old ailing man rather more feeble than himself, an idiot daughter and an orphan grand-daughter, all inhabiting a single room hovel dependent solely on the labour of one son, our workman Luke.

After mentioning the plight of other families in the neighbourhood, she added:

> It requires constant watching to keep them all in order – up to industry – in heart, and out of all the long catalogue of miseries poverty is heir to. The school is the foundation of all hope for their future. To waken up their faculties is the only dependence we can have for another generation of a happier kind. When I look back on the condition in which we found our pretty little property I can hardly believe that fifteen years should or could have worked out so improved a state of things. Land neglected, mud hovels, ruined farm offices wanting, proper fences unknown, meat seldom tasted, rags for clothing, all in debt, in dirt, in utter ignorance of everything; this was what we met the memorable day that Pat Lalor answered my enquiry as to who were all that mob of beggars, with 'Thim's the tinants'. Now we have larger farms, larger fields, some good fences, much finer cattle, a few sheep, even some turnips, five new slated houses, three of them two storeys high, good clothing, meal and bread and bacon and a 'bit of beef by times'. Draining a rage, planting, clearing, good schools, a night school, lending library, and much approach towards cleanliness. Fifteen years more and what may we not hope for.

Shortly after this, one of the servants announced her forthcoming marriage to a local man which prompted the following entry:

> Were they to wait a few years, it would be a desirable connection for them both. As it is, they have saved nothing, they are both in good places which, on their marriage, they will lose, and with the prospect of the scarcity before them from the failure of the potato crop, without a house, without employment, they are going trusting in the Lord!

* * *

The full effects of the blight were not, as yet, evident in the immediate neighbourhood of Baltiboys and Blessington. The combination of a very good general harvest and the comparative lateness in the season of the arrival of the disease in Ireland meant that less than half of the total potato crop was actually lost but it was to be some time before this became evident. In some favoured areas like Blessington, the damage caused by the blight was significantly less severe than elsewhere:

> The potato failure has been much exaggerated, the disease is by no means so far spread as was supposed and the crop so over-abundant that the partial failure will be the less felt, particularly as the corn harvest was excellent. But people were much frightened and this caused a run on the Savings Banks which might have encreased the evil, that too is luckily over so that the prospects for the winter are brightening. John Robinson said nothing could more fully prove the encreasing prosperity of the country than the multitudes whom this panick proved to have been saving, the very poorest-looking people drawing out their fortys, fiftys, hundreds. The crowds were so immense and so excited that horse and foot police were necessary to guard their lives. It was quite a curious sight.

The (British) government at the time has often been criticised for its handling of the Irish potato famine. One of the kinder reasons put forward was that it did not realise the seriousness of this hitherto unknown disease for which there was then no known antidote. The blight had struck the area around London weeks before it crossed the Irish Sea so that the actual consequences for the potato crop were already known but, for Ireland, the most serious aspect of the blight was not the disease itself but the almost complete dependence on the tuber by about one quarter of the population.

It is difficult to escape the conclusion that even if the potato blight had never happened, the system whereby something over two million of the poorest people in Ireland were subsisting on a single crop, was nothing short of a recipe for disaster. These people possessed no land of their own and were totally dependent upon the conacre system of renting land for eleven months each year. While the amount of land available under this scheme remained more or less constant, the rapidly increasing population meant that competition for the available land increased proportionately, with the inevitable result of a steady rise in the rents and/or further sub-division of the land.

As if this were not enough in itself, there was the added 'time bomb' of monoculture. The same crop was being grown year-by-year on the same plots because there simply was not enough land to allow for crop rotation which was essential to prevent the build-up of disease in the soil. A very small minority of people at the time recognised the problem but its sheer scale meant that, even if the government had wanted to change the system, any meaningful change was, given the resources then available, virtually impossible.

There was only one way out of the dilemma and that was a drastic reduction in the numbers so heavily reliant on the potato crop. Less than fifty years earlier Dr Thomas Malthus, an English economist, had expounded the theory that the population of a given area could and would, unless checked by some artificial means, such as disease, increase at a greater rate than the capacity of the available land to yield subsistence. The solution to Ireland's problem, an 'Act of God' rather than an Act of Parliament, was to prove both brutal and Malthusian.

* * *

To his credit, the prime minister, Sir Robert Peel, was aware of the problem at a very early stage and acted with commendable alacrity. Within two weeks of the first reports of the blight he had not only instigated a comprehensive survey of the Irish potato crop to be conducted on a weekly basis, an enormous undertaking in itself, but he also set up two separate commissions. The first was a relief commission to co-ordinate both the work of the special government food depots and the aid being given by landlords and the other relief committees in providing employment and cheap food. The second was a scientific commission, formed to investigate the cause of, and the means of dealing with, this hitherto unknown potato disease.

Earlier in his career, Peel had been Chief Secretary for Ireland and his knowledge of the country and its problems helped to convince him of the need to act quickly. While he was Chief Secretary, he had established the Irish constabulary, whose members came to be known as 'the peelers'. (He later organised the London police force, and also inadvertently gave his name to that force too – the 'bobbies'). Sir Robert Peel, it should be remembered, had also been largely responsible for steering the Catholic Emancipation Act through parliament.

Peel's bravest act in connection with the Irish famine was to order, on his own responsibility, supplies of Indian corn for importation to Ireland from America, a decision which proved critical in off-setting some of the effects of the crop failure during the first famine year.

A series of Acts designed to mitigate some of the worst effects of the famine were also introduced; these included the Relief of Destitute Persons

Act, which came to be known as 'the soup kitchen act'; the Poor Relief Act, which Elizabeth thought would 'ruin peasantry and landlords but others think it will work in the most effective manner'; and the Public Works Act which authorised the setting up of county relief works.

Various voluntary bodies tried to help, perhaps most notably the Religious Society of Friends, 'the Quakers', and also the British Association for the Relief of Extreme Distress in the Remote Parishes of Ireland and Scotland – a reminder that parts of Scotland were severely affected too. Not everyone in Britain was happy with the idea of spending large sums of money on Ireland: Elizabeth received a letter from the London publisher, Robert Chambers, to whom she regularly sent articles for publication, to earn what she called her 'essay money'. He was 'very angry with Ireland whose necessities have prevented the repeal of the tax on paper; the mercantile world are beginning to tire of so expensive an appendage, and incline to leave us to ourselves to fight out our own quarrels and to rely on our own resources'.

Elizabeth made a number of references to the Relief Committees. In February, 1847 she noted that: 'their sale of provisions at cost price keeps starvation from every door though it may not give plenty to every house'. These bodies, however, did not concern themselves with clothing which was a serious problem for the destitute, so Elizabeth wrote that she was going to look after her own people 'in this particular', and also to 'take charge of their gardens having sent for seeds, and to get the dung heaps removed from the doorways, have the manure dug in to the gardens, where there are any, and buy it and carry it away where there are none'. She was also determined to 'undertake an anti-tobacco mission though with little hope of success ... the poor are very extravagant, no better than the rich, human nature, full of frailties. Self is the devil, figuratively and really ... that's better gospel than we hear from the pulpits'.

Later, when the effects of the 1845 potato failure seemed less serious than first anticipated, it was decreed that the relief works were to cease as soon as the roads then in progress were completed. Elizabeth commented:

> What is to be done with the immense army of disbanded workmen is not known. The Government measures are not fully developed. Some new Irish poor law bill has passed the Commons but we don't yet know the details, nor is the Loan to the proprietors for improvements yet ready to be acted on.

She soon discovered another feature of the attempts to alleviate the distress caused by the famine:

> The relief don't reach down to the very lower class it was intended principally to succour. Most of the labourers are in debt to the hucksters, as deep as those hucksters would let them go – a week's provision is the ordinary extent. When they get their pay therefore the little shopman at whose counter the change is given, pockets it in payment for the last score while the poor victim contracts a new one to keep his family alive, his money going but a little way either, for all provisions are from 6d to 10d a stone dearer in these places than at our relief stores. The thing don't appear to have struck anybody, nor is the remedy easy; the only one that appears to me likely to succeed is to oblige the pay clerk to provide himself with change, then to put into each man's hand his few shillings which he can then spend where he pleases. To the one or two in whom we are interested we have advanced them the price of the supplies for which we gave them tickets; next pay day they will be out of the huckster's debt; they will owe us instead and they are to pay us by one shilling weekly, still leaving them an odd seven shillings in hands. Hal must represent this matter at the next meeting and now I shall turn my attention and my essay-money to the clothing of those connected with us.
>
> The farmers can't get a labourer to work for them even at fifteen pence a day; they prefer the road scraping at a shilling; on this they can just live and the delight of idleness overbalances the odd 3d though neither they nor their families have a stitch of clothes left almost. What a people.

Unhappily for the prime minister, and indeed for Ireland as well, Peel's well-meaning reactions eventually led to his loss of office. Precisely because the 1845 crop-failure was not as bad as had been first reported, he was to be accused of over-reaction and was ousted from government the following year with the help, ironically, of the Irish MPs led by Daniel O'Connell.

The new government which replaced that led by Peel had, as its leader, Lord John Russell, who was determined not to repeat what he saw as Peel's mistake of 'wasting public money' as a result of 'exaggerated reports from Ireland', a country which, to many English eyes, was notorious for exaggeration even at the best of times. One of the first decisions made by Russell was the cancellation of outstanding orders for American corn supplies, a decision which was to cause great hardship in Ireland.

Even so, fair-minded observers like Austin Bourke, whose work on aspects of the famine[1] cannot be ignored by anyone really interested in the

1. *The Visitation of God*, by Austin Bourke, (Cormac O Grada and Jacqueline Hill), Lilliput Press, Dublin 1993.

subject, feel that the government of the day and its representatives in Ireland *did* act, as he expressed it 'within the then accepted ideas of the limits of legitimate government action'. There were, he continued, 'failures to correct the dependence upon the potato, failures to learn the lessons of the past, there was waste, bungling and inefficiency, [and] there was "too little too late". However, genuine efforts were made and, given the sheer scale of the problem, it is unlikely that any other government, whether native or foreign, could or would have been able to do very much more.' The prompt decisions made by Peel and the introduction of the Temporary Relief of Destitute Persons Act (the latter provided relief for almost 2.3 million people) probably represented an unparalleled alteration in the thinking of any government anywhere at that time. Until then, the generally accepted attitude was that it was improper for a government to provide any form of aid to its citizens – the notion of of social welfare was light-years away.

Whatever about the government, one of the few groups to emerge from the aftermath of the famine with a totally honourable record was the Religious Society of Friends. There was a community of Quakers in Baltiboys in the seventeenth and eighteenth centuries. A meeting house had been established there in 1736, clearly marked on Jacob Neville's 1760 map of Wicklow. The last appointment of trustees to it was made in 1794. There is also a Quaker burial ground adjacent to the site of the meeting house, and Elizabeth made several passing references to it on her various visits to her tenants.. This area on the border between Baltiboys Upper and Lower was a busy crossroads at the time with the road to Black Ditches meeting Featherbed Lane, the old road to Russborough. The local Quaker community with its meeting house and graveyard, pin factory and Weavers' Square were all to be found here.

Among the Quakers in County Wicklow and nearby East Kildare there were several Smith families, which would appear to beg the question whether or not Colonel Smith's family might, at some period, have been one of them. In fact, there does not appear to be any evidence that this was the case and, furthermore, the Quaker records of burials at Baltiboys indicate that no Smiths were buried there between 1684 and 1809 – the first and last interments. That Elizabeth seems to have shown no particular interest in the Quaker graveyard other than as a local landmark would seem to confirm there was, in fact, no family connection with the Religious Society of Friends but if evidence to the contrary should ever emerge, the compassion shown by the Smiths to their own tenants would surely fit comfortably with the still-remembered Christian benevolence shown generally by the Quakers during the famine years.

The Catholic graveyard lies in the same locality on the site of an old

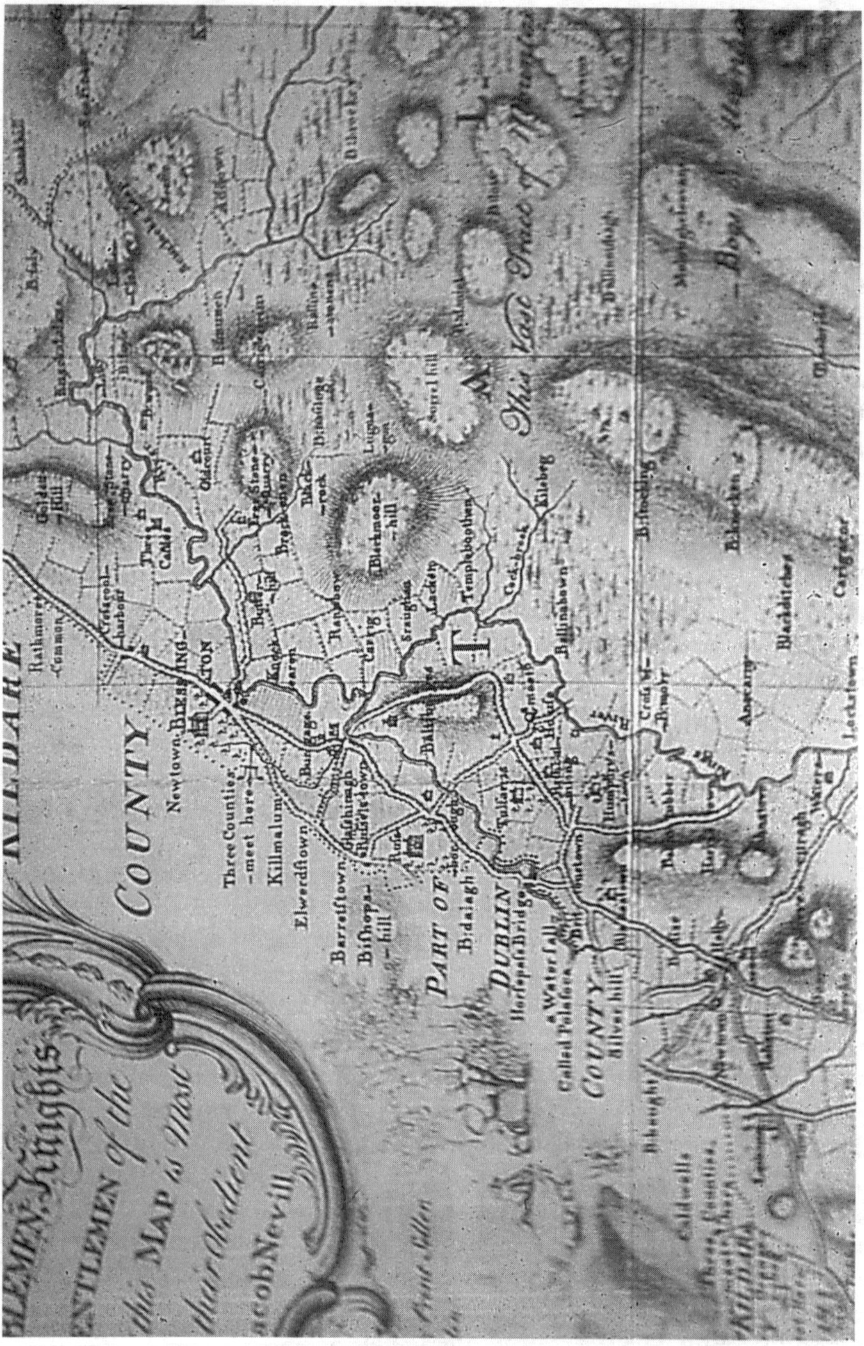

Jacob Neville's map of Wicklow, 1760, showing Baltiboys House and the Quaker Meeting House nearby.

church. A public house was situated on the corner of the cross roads, As part of the famine relief this loop in the road was bypassed by a new road, still referred to by old people in the area as the 'new line', going directly to what is now Valleymount. Featherbed Lane has all but disappeared since the valley was flooded by the reservoir.

Elizabeth Smith, after reading the news that Peel had resigned as Prime Minister, wondered:

> What the country will do without the only common-sense head in it, remains for time to show; it will require no common talents to steer our unwieldy vessel through so many shallows.

To her great relief, two weeks later Elizabeth read that the prime minister had been recalled after Russell, the leader of the Whig party, failed to form an administration. For Peel this was only a temporary reprieve and, sadly for Ireland, Russell was to oust Peel and his party the following year.

* * *

In her final entry for 1845, Elizabeth wrote that if ever anyone had reason to look back over the preceding twelve months with satisfaction it should be her:

> ... for our little circle in this wide universe has had but blessings to commemorate. All we love that are left to us are well, our home thriving, place progressing, people improving, neighbours agreeable, children our comfort. Hal is not as young as he was, which is hardly extraordinary considering that in March next he will be sixty-six; for this age he is a strong man, active, cheerful and hardy; he must not expect to do all that he has done. For me, my health seems to be gradually returning to me. We are certain of nothing and I still feel great prudence to be necessary, but with prudence I hope yet to see a few years and to pass them not uselessly.

Two photographs taken at Baltiboys around 1900. (Above): The old avenue to the house, lined by trees planted by Colonel Smith about 60 years earlier. (Below): The back elevation of Baltiboys House, with the wooded lower slopes of Baltiboys Hill on the right. (Patricia Pelly)

1846

"Here comes the famine"

Early in the new year, Elizabeth Smith's journal recorded the death of one of the pupils from the local school. The child's uncle had been home for Christmas from Birkenhead, and after he contracted scarlet fever he had died:

> ... so they waked him in form, Mrs John Fitzpatrick taking her three children to the infected house, a place the size of a sofa, and keeping them up all night in the crowd round the corpse. Little Jane sickened the second day and was brought home in the cold morning air without one wrap about her.

The end result of this was that 'dear little pretty Peggy Fitzpatrick', as she called her, died and the school children 'attended her remains to the grave, her own class walking immediately behind the coffin'.

Following the funeral of a child of another tenant who died during the following year, this time it was 'poor little Andy Ryan', Elizabeth wrote that:

> ... these unfortunate parents; they have now but three children left of ten, and their only girl will hardly long survive for she is a wretched looking little creature. Between constitutional delicacy, the great dung heap at their door, the mother's carelessness, and the father's aversion to go in time for the Doctor, they have lost a fine clever family. This was a particularly talented boy of twelve whom we intended to bring up as a national school teacher; he went to the fair of Naas, caught cold on a neglected stomach and, not attended to, got gastrick fever ending in suffusion of the brain; he died in strong convulsions yesterday morning.

More than a week later, Elizabeth added:

> I certainly got a great fright, not only with Andy Ryan's death, but on the way to Blackditches at the Carrolls' publick house and at the filthy

One of the more than 70 houses which were demolished prior to the flooding of the Liffey Valley in 1939. Many were occupied at the time by descendants of tenants of the Baltiboys Estate. (Dept of Irish Studies, UCD)

> Scarfes' every inmate was seized; however they are all off to hospital, such lime washings are going on and other purifications that the pestilence seems checked. A fine cool wind too has been blowing all round these healthy hills, and it is intended to change the food – give half rice and half Indian meal, cooked – 1 *pound* of each furnishing when properly made, made 10 *pounds* of nutritious stirabout, exceedingly good, and sufficient for a meal for four working men. We made some yesterday and to-day I have copied the printed recipe to distribute, and mean to have it further spread by the school children, each of whom shall write a copy to carry home. We made in like manner copies of the white-washing order and pasted them up in several conspicuous places. They are all allowed, with their families, to keep their rations while in the bog, cutting *their own* turf; this ensures comfort next winter, and by the time this work is over the hay and the turnip weeding will be on.

Several years before this, the journal recorded a very different kind of funeral which had taken place from Baltiboys House following what Elizabeth described as 'the dear children's first sorrow':

> ... their canary bird is dead. He was killed by the cat, who had stolen into the room and concealed herself under the bed. so she had the whole night to worry her victim. It was hard to comfort Jack. All were in tears to Miss Cooper and Caroline, for Dickey was a great pet, so tame that he flew about the room, fed from their hands, sat on their

> heads or hands or shoulders. He was buried under a rose tree in a coffin and wrapped in flannel – a very melancholy procession of maids and children bore the loved remains to the grave, and the tears that fell were many and most sincerely shed. Nobody speaks of him, mirth is gone and the cat entirely out of favour – she was publickly whipped by the side of the cage and is banished to the kitchen.

Returning to the subject of the introduction of Indian corn flour, which was one of the emergency measures taken by the government in an attempt to alleviate the failure of the potato crop, Elizabeth wrote:

> The Doctor brought us yesterday a printed paper, published by Government to teach the people how to use the Indian corn flour. It will be very useful although the Dutch oven part might have been left out, even a griddle few of the poor possess, and to talk of yeast and butter and eggs and new milk to perfect paupers is a sort of mockery. Margaret and I can teach the porridge, the hasty pudding and the common cakes from seeing them made at Pau [in France] where the maize flour is much used. Unfortunately any trouble is so disagreeable to the habits of our indolent population, I doubt their taking it till actually dying from want, any food they are unaccustomed to they dislike equally, but the famine is coming, has begun in the plains and must reach the hills, and though those immediately belonging to our small knot of good landlords may feel little of it, all around are already in misery, the poor broom man among them who, while walking up from the gate with me, his load upon his back, told me he had no work, no food, and was reduced to one meal a day, himself, his wife and five children. Why will they marry on nothing ?

In May the Smith family and some friends had a picnic on Blackamore Hill where they enjoyed the panorama, drank tea, 'danced the polka', and passed a merry evening. The diary entry described the scene as it ended:

> One of the pleasantest sights of the day was our group of attendants [going] over the fragments – men who never taste meat twice in a year truly enjoying what we had left of our luxuries; the saddest was one the Doctor and young John Hornidge called me to look at – a little ragged frightened boy, the herd of some cattle grazing on these uplands who had collected on a stone the shakings out of the table cloth, and who was piling up crusts of bread with one hand and holding bare bones to his mouth with the other – the impersonation of famine. Need I set out that we added more substantial morsels to his store – enough too for

> the morrow, and the Doctor slipt sixpence into the poor thin hand for milk hereafter.

On the following day, 'another day of misery', she wrote that the Doctor had got a note from old John Hornidge to go and visit a tenant, Edward Shannon:

> My mind misgave me that the man was dying, like his children, of starvation so when the riders departed, the Colonel, Janey [Elizabeth's elder daughter] and I drove over to see; the one room was very clean, almost tidy, except for a stack of furze at the foot of the bed – the fuel. The man was lying down ill enough, the wife burst into tears when I entered. 'Now God be praised', she said, 'we are saved'. 'Oh Lady Smith, my jewel', etc. He had worked on, when quite unfit for labour, because his wages are stopt in sickness; he gets ninepence a day, but having two acres of ground and this miserable cabin so much is stopt for rent as leaves him but two shillings a week in money. He sublet his land to pay for firing, he sold his cow to pay his debts, and there he is with six children, five of them girls, and one an idiot. Their potatoes being done for a fortnight they have had in the family but one meal a day; no wonder the children had no spirit at their lessons. Yesterday morning they had nothing till the old grandmother Mrs Delany sent them two quarts of meal from her scanty store. Biddy Shannon made two halves of this – one half gave them all a cup of thick gruel yesterday; to-day it was thin as she had to keep enough for a drink in the evening for her husband; the little girls wept bitterly. Oh how they bounded off for milk and meal when the means to get both were given to them.

Next day, after sending broth to the sick tenant, she expected that he should 'recover if well fed'.

Elizabeth always wrote in the most affectionate terms about her old highland home at The Doune, Rothiemurchus, and it was around this time that she spent three weeks there during a Scottish holiday.

> In spite of all the changes nineteen years have seen, many of the old friends of my youth are still here to welcome me back among them; the children of a few others are grown up full of the recollections of their parents; so it a'n't all melancholy that has met me in the home of my youth.

Her coach had been met by Willie the ostler, who looked after the horses. 'Right glad he was to welcome me back, for tears stood in the poor man's eyes'. On the very next day, she set out on her favourite walk through the forest behind the house to the little Loch an Eilein – the same route that she and her sister had walked on the last day before the family had to leave for India in 1827. After visiting many other well-remembered places and the relations and friends who lived there, her sadness at having to leave the Highlands once more is clearly demonstrated in her journal entry: 'Breakfasted early, filled Mr McCaw's cart; a melancholy procession, and all mourned the end of so many happy weeks'.

In June, 1846, the Smith's estate agent, John Robinson, collected the half-year rents, and Elizabeth recorded that the tenants paid well 'generally':

> No complaints except from the sickness among the cattle some time ago which was a serious misfortune. The scarcity of potatoes is little felt by the farmers it being caused principally by the stocks being kept back from the markets in the expectation of prices rising continually which system pressed heavily on the labouring purchasers in which class the failure of the crop has been the commonest owing to inferiour management ....

Elizabeth then went on to remark that 'the passing of the corn bill has lowered all provisions already'. This was a reference to the Repeal of the Corn Laws in 1846, an Act introduced by Peel despite the fact that some time before, he had pledged not to do so. The effect of the Act was to lift all the protectionist duties that had been imposed on imported grain which did, in fact, reduce the price of bread but its effectiveness, as far as the poor were concerned, was largely off-set by the fact that many of them could not afford bread even at the reduced price. Other measures introduced included the already mentioned importation of Indian corn but even the starving, probably because they did not know what to do with it, found it to be virtually inedible.

A Relief Commission was set up which gave employment in return for work, often on the roads, but the government began to take the view that it was the landlords who had the first duty to look after their tenants. Many landlords took a very different view and availed of the opportunity to rid themselves of unwanted or troublesome tenants either by eviction or by encouraging them to emigrate. Some landowners, however, made genuine efforts to help their tenants, forming local relief committees, distributing food and even foregoing rents. The Smiths of Baltiboys were certainly in this latter category but this did not prevent them from being highly critical of those whom they judged to be unwilling to make some effort on their own behalf. In September, 1846, Elizabeth wrote:

> I can't hear of much change among our people; Ned Gray married, his wife brought home to three acres of course. Old Mrs Quin, the mother of Red Pat, dead. The whooping cough has been very prevalent, in some cases where fever was superadded, fatal. The potato crop gone, here and everywhere, the root I suppose extinct, and were we once over this first year may be 'tis so best, for the cheapness of this low description of food encouraged idleness, pauper marriages and dirty habits, and neither mind nor body could be fully developed upon such nourishment. Government is exerting itself nobly to provide useful work with good pay, therefore like last year the Irish labourer will fare well. All summer, hands have been so scarce from the number required by the railroads and the new buildings that the farmers have been paying from 1/6 to 2/6 a day with diet, good bread, greens, milk, bacon, pork, etc., yet no one is satisfied – all miss the potatoes. Even old Peggy is all lamentation, no other food is so strengthening.

On several occasions Elizabeth noted that while some of their neighbours, such as George Moore, Mr Armstrong and Richard Hornidge, did what they could for the poor, other resident landlords, as she put it:

> get on in the old ways, the lowest wages, little work, no help in advice or otherwise; they may throw about a few pence when importuned by beggars, but they will take no trouble – they will not do justice. And there are large tracts of land belonging to absentees filled with squatters – all paupers – among whom a shilling is never spent, and who, with the neglected peasantry of the indolent landlords, are all thrown upon us the willing horses.

Unlike the year before, the blight in 1846 began in the west and then spread eastwards. More ominously, the disease started two months earlier and in some cases the crop had been destroyed by early August. By September it had become obvious that the potato crop was doomed to be an even worse failure than that of the year before and Ireland was about to face the most intense period of hardship seen in any of the famine years. Towards the end of the month, Elizabeth noted the effects as they became apparent around her in Baltiboys:

> Here comes the famine too, the rain has spoiled the few miserable potatoes left, the markets are higher than they were ever known to be since the [Napoleonic] war; work is over; the Irish landlords generally are bankrupt, three fourths of the land mortgaged to full value with, therefore, nominal large rent rolls they have not a penny to spend in

labour. From some hitch between the government and the Board of Works, no publick works are going forward, the ministry don't choose to interfere with the provision trade; so here we are, the peasantry starving.

On the following day she returned to this theme:

This was the day for a meeting of the gentry, etc. in Blesinton, to consider the state of the starving poor, two or three hundred of whom collected in the village to learn the result which appeared to be simply that they would be looked after; at least I could make very little else out of the rambling account the Doctor gave us of the proceedings. The Act of Parliament is so imperfect it don't at all meet the emergency and, it is supposed, the collective wisdom of the nation must assemble without delay to amend it, for as it stands those landlords who have always done, are now doing and intend to continue to do their duty, will be assessed for the support of those of the lower orders who have been neglected by bad landlords, who again having never done anything for their people will get them all supported now as a recompense for their improper carelessness, the willing horse in fact, having to bear the burden even till his back be broke. It seems however that there is some way of exempting oneself from this overweight by the landlord giving his own pledge to employ all able-bodied persons on his property, or to see them employed, and to send the incapables to the poor house. Mr Moore, Mr Armstrong and Mr Owen have thus exempted themselves, and as we have not only all our people occupied but three or four strangers in addition we must get some 'voice' to speak for Lower Baltiboys as poor Hal is at present too unwell to attend any of the meetings. It seems very unwise in the Government to refuse to interfere with the provision trade, for the capitalists are buying up all the grain to retail really at an exorbitant price – two and eight pence a stone for meal. I have known it a shilling, two and threepence for wheatmeal. What labourer's wages can support his family at these rates, and how can wages rise when there are double the number of workmen that are wanted. Something must be done for, between the poverty of the masters and the destitution and the idleness and the recklessness of the people, mischief will most certainly ensue if matters are left to take their own course.

A couple of days later, Elizabeth recorded that she and the estate steward, Tom Darker, spent the whole morning 'settling affairs'. She went on:

> He has dismissed the two old men who, for the present, have work elsewhere. James Doyle will most likely get enough during the winter to support his family, a brother in America having lately sent him £10, and written for the eldest son to go out to him. James Craig and his dirty idle wife must take their wretched children to the Poor House, old John Doyle may want a little help, so may Pat Quin's delicate mother, no one else. And instead of raising wages, a bad precedent, the Colonel with pleasure consents to give them meal at a low price instead of selling his oats in the market and, to ensure his supply lasting, the horses will get none unless the two working mares one feed each. Then we shall buy another cow, and so have milk all winter to divide amongst them. Thus we hope to get through this famine year, and being able to pledge ourselves to the good work, Tom will go to Mr Owen and get us exempted from all care of our neighbours.

And later still she wrote that while several of the other landlords in the locality were prepared to help the poorer people, 'Lord Palmerston [is] playing the very mischief, and our wretched peasantry are actually starving while these wiseheads are battling how to relieve them'.

* * *

During a short visit to Oxford in October 1846, she could not help noticing the rich fields and neat villages, the clean cottages, the bright windows, the good clothing, and the general air of comfort, all of which contrasted so starkly with County Wicklow. Seeing a newspaper report that provisions were continuing to pour into England from Ireland, she commented that it appeared from this that food must be plentiful in Ireland and once again blamed the plight of many on their idleness. 'They have got it into their heads that being in distress they are to do nothing to get out of it, but are to sit comfortably down and open their mouths to be fed.' She added: 'I can't but despise a people so uninspired, so low-minded, so totally without energy, only I attribute it to the want of animal food'.

* * *

Back in Ireland a few weeks later she found the political news just as dreary. 'Nothing can be more deplorable than their Irish measures, they are positively demoralising the people still further than their own bad feelings had accomplished'. Elizabeth continued to change her mind about the government's reactions to the famine, sometimes describing their efforts as 'noble', sometimes 'imperfect' or 'mismanaged' or 'too late' and, when

The Downshire Hotel, Blessington, formerly the Downshire Estate administrative office. The Marquis of Downshire stayed here during his visits to Blessington. (Séamas Ó Maitiú)

The Parish House built by Fr Germain in 1845 at Black Ditches (Valleymount). The porch is said to have been salvaged from Blessington Manor House. (Dermot James)

she was in despair, she could write that 'it is as if lunatics were legislating'.

During November, the rents were again due and, despite the general situation, their tenants had paid 'very nearly as well as usual.' She went on:

> Some require a fortnight to pay up, others will persist to owe the hanging half year. A few who should do better owe a year. One or two owe more, we therefore in earnest proceed with them. About £160 is due. All will be in time recovered little by little except poor George Kearn's encreasing arrears, he must go, and at once, for his own sake, it would have been better had he gone years ago. Redmond has paid no rent for these three gales [biannual rent audits], nor Cullen, the old man and woman have gone off to England to a prosperous son, the youngest boy has settled himself and a wife down in the cabin with its acre without leave from any one and this is extremely hard, he is not to be allowed to remain.
>
> Upon the whole we have no reason to be dissatisfied with the conduct of our people these pinching times, they will require a steady rein, kind words, encouragement in many ways and thus proceeding I think we shall get over the season better than most of us. Money will be scarce enough, by the time the Christmas bills are paid there will be no great stock remaining, but in February comes the pay again.

Snow fell at the end of the month, followed by a hard frost, which she described as 'fine healthy weather, but the starving, those who have bad shelter, scanty fire, little food, God help them for man can't. Were we to divide our all with all we could not ensure their comfort for they have ruined dwellings, they have laid in no fuel, their clothing is but rags and provisions are at triple price' This entry continues:

> Such a miserable creature as besought Janey [her elder daughter, then aged about 16] and me yesterday to buy a straw basket that she might carry home a supper to four children and a husband who had fasted with herself since the night before. He has got [to work] upon the roads but will not be paid till the pay day, nor then in full, as the overseers are obliged to keep this bridle over these wretched idlers, and how to subsist these two days the half distracted creature knew not. 'Oh Lady Smith, my jewel' said she, sobbed she rather, 'sound may ye sleep on your feather pillow for all belonging to you is in comfort. Long life to his honour, for it is he that's the father to his people. If others were like him and looked to their own there would not be this famine in the country'.

> I have made up my mind that the distress of the poor demands a large sacrifice on the part of the richer, and it must be our business to prepare for this and to give up luxuries to meet this. 'To feed the hungry' is a duty that cannot be shirked and Hal is not inclined to shirk it. He will find his whole family anxious to second his right intentions, willing to bear their share of the difficulties, and as Almighty God never fails to fit the back to the burden, by His blessing we may hope to get through this season of trial using the means we are but the stewards of to the best of our abilities in alleviating this great distress. The young, the aged, the weakly, must suffer, let us do our utmost, for the able bodied, though employed, can't earn sufficient for their support while provisions are so unnaturally high and this brings on the question whether the Government have acted right in declining to interfere with the markets. Extraordinary cases require extraordinary treatment. Abstract principles are probably correct and in future years may work for good, but having never acted on them hitherto we are not prepared to receive them, and one shudders at stepping over mounds of graves in the experiment at this time. At the present it would require 21/- [shillings] a week to support a labourer and his family, he earns 6/-,7/- or 8/- at the highest. What must be the result?

Colonel Smith went to a meeting of the Government Commission on 4 December and then to the Presentment Sessions. A friend called to the house two days later and explained to Elizabeth what had been decided:

> The money already voted has been very carefully expended even with all the jobbing, and as this will be particularly watched there are funds sufficient to meet all charges till March. We therefore are called on to do nothing more for the present. With the usual hanging on spirit of their country, the whole people of the district were crowding to seize their share of what they look on as fair plunder and fancied was Government money, regardless of the fact that their rulers and landlords were coming forward only to relieve the destitute by employing labourers whose work was not wanted and whose wages it was a serious tax to have to pay, every man with a pair of arms rushed to the roads where they scrape away in herds, lazily, carelessly, and almost uselessly. Men with several acres of ground up to twenty, or thirty even, mangers with their stores full, families with a good sum saved, sons of parents in comfortable circumstances all represented themselves as starving, and leaving their proper employments came craving for the bread belonging to the poor. Hal, had a list of men who sent asses to draw gravel, all of them able to give relief instead of requiring it, some of these asses bought, or hired cheap from those whom it was intended should have

had the benefit of them. Many of these cases having been reported and the farmers beginning to comprehend that wherever the money may come from now they will themselves in the end have to pay their share of it, and that the fewer at work the less to pay, we hope the ferment will subside and things by and bye resume their ordinary level. If provisions fall [in price], which looks likely, the distress will be much relieved. Still the sick, the weakly and the aged must be assisted, not more than usual however.

Snow fell again on 17 December to add to the general misery, but when it had disappeared by the following day Elizabeth noted that:

> The Poor Houses are full, therefore now I believe in the destitution cry. The people are starving I believe. Cold and nakedness and discomfort of every kind they are indifferent to, provided they can fill their stomacks, stuff them rather with the lowest quality of food, its bulk is what they look for, for years the failure of the potato crop has been expected, yet no preparations were made to meet this coming evil. They have no fore thought. If they get a shilling they must spend it. They can't make 11d do and save the penny, they have no store for the rainy day, then when it comes they rail at all the rest of the world for not stepping forward to their relief instantly as if they deserved the quicker aid because they never helped themselves. There is no energy, no honesty, no industry among them. But this wide spread calamity must rouse them. Already good effects have been produced. The Poor House will improve their habits, the dearness of provisions has driven many of the idle hangers-on at home out into the world to earn the food no longer to be had by grubbing for it. So we must live in hope that, happen what may, things can never again be so wretchedly bad as they have been.

On 20 December the weather had turned milder and Elizabeth's doctor-friend told her that:

> The famine has come, is in every house on Bishop Hill, Pinmaker's Hill, Hollywood and the Radcliffes mountains. Every neglected property, in short; the Poor House is full, 1,100 where there never was 200, and sheds erecting for hundreds more; the price of provisions is so enormous, three times the wages would not give sufficient food to a family. After Christmas soup kitchens must be set up.
>
> We have been trying rice and find it liked so have sent for a further supply although we cannot get it so cheap in a small quantity in Dublin as it could be got in Liverpool or as we hope to get it shortly from John Robinson, who has been written to by a London house on the subject, they offer it at from 13/6 to 16/- the cwt. We are paying 24/- and even

The home of Pat Ryan, a carpenter and one of the Baltiboys tenants, where he lived with his brother James. (Séamas Ó Maitiú)

Bryan Dempsey, who was one of the 'difficult' tenants, lived in this house, described by Elizabeth as 'a good new house, dry and light'. (Séamas Ó Maitiú)

> at that price it is the cheapest food to be had. Old Peggy sells it at 3d a lb. and sold a stone a day the two first days when few knew she had it, so we have ordered 2 cwt, and we will order a ton if necessary, and buy coarse beef which Peggy can make into soup to sell at cost price or below it where needful.

Bishop's Hill, mentioned above, is close to Ballymore Eustace. Pinmakers Hill took its name from the former pin-making factory near Weavers Square, and the Radcliffe mountains were named after a middleman who had leased land in the hills south east of Baltiboys.

* * *

On the last day of the year, she wrote:

> The end of a happy year ... during which we have had as much pleasure and suffered as little pain as could possibly fall on the lot of humanity. Except that the Colonel and I are growing old [Elizabeth was then 50] we have little personal to complain of.... For the present however I mean to keep myself young a while. I have much work to do and I must not let indolence unfit me for my labours. Farewell 1846.

1847

"Alas, the famine progresses"

Early in the new year the Smiths proposed 'dabbling in the provision line', establishing their own store for the purpose of supplying the neighbouring poor at a reasonable price, and Elizabeth returned to the subject of rice:

> We have begun with rice, which old Peggy retails for us at 3d per lb., getting a ready sale hitherto. By and bye we shall have it for them cheaper as John Robinson has contracted with a London house for a supply to arrive in April at a much lower rate than we can get it now. We are also thinking of adding a little Indian meal to our stock; unfortunately in all our range of offices there is no storeroom for grain, etc. but I think we could manage to make one. The repository continues to thrive quietly. Whenever the poor women have a sixpence to lay out on themselves or their children they go there for their clothing, but of course this hard year they have less to spend in this way than usual. The schools are all to begin again. We hope we have at last procured a family to suit us. An elderly man, married, with daughters capable of undertaking the charge of the female children. Miss Gardiner [the former teacher] went very nearly out of her mind when she found she was really dispensed with, and actually thinks she has been very harshly treated, turned out of doors in fact because, after the fifth resignation, she was taken at her word.
>
> She has by no means given me satisfaction for some time past. We can't fail to change for the better. All the 'Busy Bees' fully occupied, for this honey making insect is all alive again. It is delightful to feel useful once more. Unfortunately I can't go about much out of doors, but I manage to know what is doing.
>
> New Year's Day being fine the girls and I paid many visits and all the houses we entered showed much humble comfort. Would that all around us were the same. However charity must begin at home, quite certain of not ending there. Example does much and as we can't assist

> all we must only continue to look after our own and be content to distribute elsewhere the crumbes left by those who have a right to the bread. We are giving milk and soup to all our workmen and soup to all our sick or aged. Margaret has a large pot of soup ready every day at one o'clock and a list of persons to whom she has to give it. Each gets a quart every second day. At present we have to give twelve quarts daily. The workmen have milk on the day they don't get soup, and we must buy another cow for we are running short both of milk and butter. Upon consultation with Mr Darker the Colonel adopted this plan in preference to that of raising wages. The poor are such bad managers, they spend their money very foolishly and in the matter of food which supplies the strength on which the breadwinner works, the women are so ignorant, so indolent, that they are utterly incapable of preparing a comfortable meal. They have not fuel indeed to cook one, nor pot nor pan not griddle nor crock to prepare one in, most of them at least.

Elizabeth, as can be seen, often balanced her compassion with quite harsh criticism and she sometimes despaired of the unfortunate poor people around her as many journal entries demonstrate. A few days later she was in such a mood:

> Alas! the famine progresses; here it is in frightful reality to be seen in every face. Idle, improvident, reckless, meanly dependant on the upper classes whom they so abuse; call the bulk of the Irish what we will, and no name is too hard almost for them, here they are starving round us, cold, naked, hungry, well nigh houseless. To rouse them from their natural apathy may be the work of future years. To feed them must be our business this. Baltiboys is in comfort, few of our people in real distress, some in want of assistance and they get it, others in need of nothing. My habit of going constantly about among them keeps me pretty well acquainted with their condition, but lest I should miscalculate I am taking the whole estate regularly through at this time. Two days of visiting introduced me to no distress, only to two cases of struggling – that expressive word. I mean to make a catalogue *raisonne* of our population to leave among our family archives as a curiosity for future squires and a guide to us now.
>
> Hal has killed a beef for our poor and we make daily a large pot of good soup which is served gratis to 22 people at present. It is ready at one o'clock and I thought it quite a pretty sight yesterday in the kitchen all the workmen coming in for their portion, a quart with a slice of the beef; half of them get this one day for a dinner with a bit of their own

bread; the other half get milk and the cheap rice we have provided for them. Next day they reverse the order. The Colonel is giving them firing too; so they are really comfortable; there are twelve of them and ten pensioners, old feeble men and women, or those with large families of children; some of them no longer living on our ground yet once having been connected with us we can't desert them.

So far well; but beyond our small circle what a waste of misery; how are we to relieve it? Such a dense population squatted here and there upon neglected properties, dying with want, wretched every year, but ruined this. At the Relief Committee yesterday it was resolved to institute soup kitchens at proper stations for general relief, to be supported by subscription, each subscriber to have a certain number of tickets. I think the gentlemen doing this, the ladies must combine for clothing fund. The rags are scarcely coverings for decency; beds and bedding there are none, among the mob I mean; such misery crushes hope, yet hope I will. 'Hope and Wait' as was Dante's motto.

Elizabeth drew up for herself a daily routine of visiting on foot whenever the weather was fine or, on 'middling days' taking 'the little covered carriage'. For her, every walk or drive had an object; a farm, the repository, a sick call, etc., and when the weather was bad she busied herself around the house with the storeroom, the workroom, the accounts, the garden, the provision stores and so on. 'Who would exchange for this rational furthering of the human race', she asked, 'the life of a town fine lady?'

Here follows a quite remarkably detailed account of a series of visits to all the tenants, extending over a period of five days, which she divided into 'walks' around the Baltiboys estate in January, 1847:

* * *

Walk the 1st:
To old Paddy and Peggy Dodson, pensioners in a good cabin near our gate which we built for them; two rooms well furnished; a good garden; their two children off their hands: Anthony a carpenter, Mary, housemaid at Rusboro'; pensions eight pounds a year. Peggy keeps the Repository and gets a penny out of every shilling's worth she sells; also keeps the cheap provision store, gets a penny for every stone weight she sells. An orphan girl is boarded with her for whose keep she gets four pounds a year; I providing clothing. We give this family soup one day, milk the next, dripping every Sunday.

James Ryan the carpenter, a good two storey, slated house with four rooms, a closet, and dairy, workshop, shed, yard, three acres of land, one apprentice, one journeyman, a boy, a maid, wife and five children;

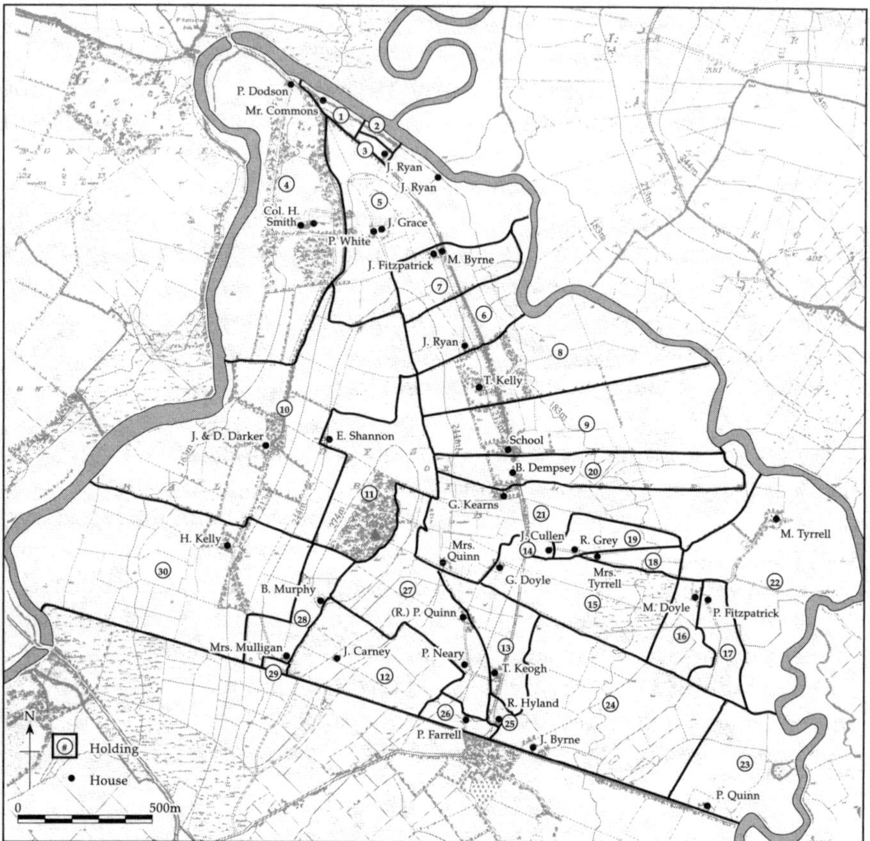

No.	Name	Acreage	No.	Name	Acreage
1.	Michael Delaney	4.5	16.	Joan Doyle	12.0
2.	Widow Darker	3.0	17.	Widow Fitzpatrick	14.0
3.	Widow Darker to Peter Nowlan	1.0	18.	Michael Tyrrell	5.0
4.	John and Thomas Darker	94.0	19.	Richard Grey	11.5
5.	Joseph and Michael Commons	74.0	20.	Bryan Dempsey and George Kearns late Dobson and Neary	32.5
6.	Christopher Ryan	22.0	21.	George Kearns late Widow Healy	67.0
7.	Patrick Ryan	22.5	22.	Michael Tyrrell	76.0
8.	Thomas Kelly	59.0	23.	Patrick Quinn	40.0
9.	Thomas Kelly late Kearns	62.5	24.	Michael Byrne	77.5
10.	John and Thomas Darker	121.0	25.	Margaret Hyland	2.0
11.	John and Thomas Darker	44.0	26.	Patrick Farrell	5.0
12.	William Quinn	38.5	27.	Col. Smith late Patrick Quinn	38.0
13.	Widow Keogh	21.0	28.	John Williams to William Morgan	17.0
14.	James Cullen	1.5	29.	John Williams to Catherine Doyle	1.0
15.	Widow Doyle	40.5	30.	John Williams to Hugh Kelly	118.5

Map of the Baltiboys estate c.1847 with which it is possible to trace the comprehensive series of visits made by Elizabeth to all the tenants. (Matthew Stout) one boy and two girls at school, two little girls mere babies. All comfortable here, neater than the general. Two cabins together on what was Judy Ryan's ground. The stableman John Fitzpatrick in one, the ploughman Miles Byrne in the other, two rooms, a large garden, a yard each, Miles a turf house; wife dead, leaving him three boys and a nurse child, a girl now at twelve years of age managing his most tidy household under the aunts, as she calls them, Mary and Betty Hyland who look in every day, these good women have also taken the two baby boys home leaving Miles only his eldest son, a clever child at school.

John Fitzpatrick's wife is neither so clean nor so tidy as her little neighbour but she has plenty in the rough, and but three children, one girl at school, two little boys, babies and a nephew of her husband's, the child of very distressed parents whom they have taken out of charity. The wages of these two men seven shillings a week with milk or soup daily. Pat Ryan a small farm of thirteen acres in high order; the lower part drained on the new system, fully stocked; poor looking house with three rooms, plenty of rude comfort, stables, sheds, etc. A wife, a mother, a half idiot brother; three boys, one Mathew in our garden just going as apprentice to Riccarton [Elizabeth's sister's home] the second assisting the father, both attending the evening school; the third a first rate boy at school; the little girl at school. Nothing wanting here. A cabin at hand is occupied by our herd and our gardener, one room each, no garden; wages seven shillings. Paddy White, the gardener has an industrious wife, no children. John Grace, the herd, a pattern of a wife and two pretty little baby girls. Both families get soup or milk daily and are very comfortable.

Next farm, ninety acres, Tom Kelly, an old man now, with old untidy ways, married at fifty a girl with a hundred pounds who has made him an excellent wife. They have a large yard, new good offices, a garden, house of three large rooms, and seven children, four boys and three girls; the four elder ones at school, plenty here but in an uncomfortable manner and the worst farming though the rent is never behind; no draining, no turnips, not sufficient stock. Hal means to resume about twenty acres of the low ground to reclaim himself as this stupid old creature can't be moved to exertion and we shall have a world of plague to get back the possession, both husband and wife acting tragedy when informed of it although they got this addition to their old holding on the express understanding of improving it.

Here ended my first day's survey which I consider very satisfactory both as to the present and future, for Tom Kelly will manage fewer acres better as he will not diminish his labourers and they are too few for the size of his present farm – two old half useless men and a little boy, all of whom he gets at half wages, with a niece as maid-servant. His little daughter, one of my pets, manages her younger brothers and sisters. The herd and gardener want each another room, one house more in fact, with garden ground, this is no year for building even a cabin – ten or twelve pounds at the cheapest to be decent, and all we can raise must go into the soup pot this miserable season We ought to have the lodge for the gardener, but that would cost much more. Patience.

* * *

Walk the second.
Next poor George Cairns – almost a fool – simple as a child and really almost as innocent, evil not in him nor good either. It is him we have taken his ground from, although he has not yet given up possession. We are waiting till we get a place for him as sawyer, the trade he was bred to, and we give him leave to retain the house for his family till he settles elsewhere; he has let his house of three rooms go to ruin, ditte [ditto] the crazy offices, bad at the best and few of them. He has not a hoof on the land, not a hen even; the hay is in small cocks on the meadow just fit for manure; fences all broken, no gates, no furniture, but decent clothing, a good bed, fuel, and corn enough to feed wife and six children till May; four fine boys are at school; a cousin lives with them who for reasons of his own has tried to prop them up these several years, but it won't do; two years' rent owing now, and the ground destroyed. They will be rich on their guinea a week, sawyer's wages, and this is utter misery; besides the wife may do her duty to George Cairns better when separated from the cousin Charles.

Close to these wretched people is a thriving farmer on the same quantity of land about thirty acres – Bryan Dempsey, a reckless, ruthless, vapouring, 'cute' model of the bad style of Irishman whom I can't feel interested in for his want of principle; two sons, two daughters, one man and an active wife compose his family; slated house with three rooms, and decent offices, clean and rather orderly, but no 'English neatness.' On again was Tom Kiogh doing well on twelve acres, but all in dirt and filth and wet; his once beautiful wife a regular old beldam, dirty beyond idea, yet all her clothes were good; her four fine boys were well dressed; three of them go to school. There was a new press, new shoes, great coats, tea things, yet the whole looked wretched from the filth. It was the dirtiest house and yard we saw, not excepting Garrett Doyle's a little above on the hill. This smart young man has a large farm forty acres or thereabouts and his fields are in good order; but his yard is knee deep with mud, offices mere ruins, house little better though the old mother keeps plenty about it. Three men and a nurse grown up into a servant maid compose this establishment which will never be more comfortable while the old woman lives. Dempsey's was by far the neatest household we saw this day; his daughters who were kept assiduously at school while they were young have acquired habits of neatness there with a perfect knowledge of their needle which has enabled them to improve their humbler home. The good new house too aids them; dry and light, they see their way and their labours of cleanliness are not in vain. A little grandchild here is going to school.

* * *

Walk the third.
Down the lane towards the King's River on the right a small cabin of three rooms, warm and clean with tidy furniture, good bedding, a neat small yard enclosed, cowhouse and pigstye. Here with one acre of ground a decent labouring man has struggled through his laborious life and reared a large family in the days of pigs and potatoes. But times are changed. James Cullen and his dear old wife are past seventy years of age; neither can work as they used to do, and the acre of ground for which they have paid no rent for the three last half years is an encumbrance to them. Still I doubt their giving it up but by and bye I shall try, though one can't be hard on the old couple. He has always made a good deal of money by preparing turf in summer for which he gets a ready sale in winter. I think of setting him up as turf merchant to the district, by lending him in spring the small capital necessary to buy a stretch of bog, an ass, and small cart; he is near the bog and the new system of farming coming in will leave the active farmer no time for cutting his own fuel. This old pair are on the soup list and James having work at his brother-in-law Michael Tyrrel's, they will get on pretty well. They would have got on quite well but for their youngest son who married against their consent, brought home his wife, robbed them right and left, and had to be bribed to leave them, the Colonel giving a pound to be rid of such a scape-grace.

To the left a better cabin and very neat yard full of manure made up properly; a cowhouse, stack of corn and hay – the produce of three acres which old Dick Gray is to keep while he lives – no long term of tenure apparently for he is in bed in a very bare room, laying upon straw, full of pains and aches, his eldest son beside him in an equally hopeless state. It was quite affecting. John Gray had been working in Liverpool under a mason to whom his elder sister is married, neglected a cold, and came home to die, poor lad, I fear; the youngest son Ned took the opportunity of these troubles and a bad season and our absence in England to get himself married. I found the wife pinned up behind a blanket in the wide kitchen chimney and recommended her and Ned who was thrashing in the kitchen, to provide themselves with a more permanent home as soon as convenient for that they were quite too many here, an unmarried daughter Kitty being the best manager for the old father whom with the sick son we added to the soup list.

In more wet and dirt and filth and misery than we had yet seen we found the next little farmer Michael Doyle, a fine looking and very hard working though low feeling man who for his sins and for her fifteen pounds, married the widow Ryan, my Annie's nurse. Her three children, two she has had since this marriage, a nurse child of course, all seem to squat on the floor of a very small kitchen, for we saw no stools, chairs, tables, nor any furniture but a crazy dresser with very little upon its shelves.

She stood to receive us in her cloke having but one gown which was washing; all the children nearly naked, the husband very bare; no way of getting up to the house but over the dung hill. She would not let me into the bedroom and then she told me they had turned it into a cowhouse and the reason the floor was so bad was that the cows passed and repassed through the kitchen. Twice I have succeeded in improving this most slatternly Judy, and twice she has fallen hack when my watchful eye was removed. I will try again – her and the husband together – rouse them if possible for they want but method to be comfortable. They have near eight acres of land, two milch cows giving her now four lbs of butter a week which she sells in the market for eleven pence a lb.; a pound she keeps and all the buttermilk; they have two young heifers coming on, and he has promised this year to sow an acre of turnips. They have still eight barrels of oats; he will want three for seed; he promises to change this at the market, to sell three of the remaining barrels, oats are very high now, twenty-four shillings a barrel, and to purchase with their price, rice and Indian meal to mix with the oatmeal his two left barrels will give. As he has just recovered from a long illness, six weeks of typhus fever which took all their spare money, the family is put on the soup list; he has had a meat dinner daily since he was able for it, and is so grateful that I hope he will oblige me by setting to work in earnest to encrease his comforts. I ordered the second girl and two little ones off to school, leaving the eldest whom we have well educated, to help her mother and mind the baby.

Close at hand was another small farm about the same size with a low bad house, very dark having no window in the kitchen, but it was a real pleasure to enter so decent an abode. Manure at one end banked up,

'The Darkers' excellent house', where Tom, the Colonel's steward, lived with his brother, two sisters and five orphan nieces and nephews. (Séamas Ó Maitiú)

The Old Toll House, Blessington. The Turnpike Trust set up in 1829 to maintain the Dublin to Baltinglass Road was abolished by an Act of Parliament in 1855. (Séamas Ó Maitiú)

cowhouse with four cows in it never let out, feeding on turnips, large turf stack, very clean kitchen, bright fire, dresser well filled, wall hung with polished pots and covers, meal chest, table, and two neat chairs brought from the bedroom and wiped with a clean cloth before being offered to us by a young pretty woman in appearance like a tidy housemaid who was churning when we came in. She was a mountain beauty with a little money and is seemingly a prize to Pat Fitzpatrick who was a widower with one child when he went to the highlands. Nothing wanted here but a praise and some little present for an encouragement. It was a real scene of humble comfort.

Close to the river rises the new two storey slated house just built by little Michael Tyrrell, the largest farmer on the property having close upon a hundred acres; a thriving man with a wife deserving of him; the offices are to follow; in the meanwhile the old steading serves the turn; the daughters of this house are all well married, the sons in trades, except the youngest Philip, who will worthily succeed his father. Last summer this fine old man when busy in his hayfield told us it was his birthday – seventy six. This day I found him in his bed where he has lain three weeks with influenza, declining he says, in want of stimulant, said I; so I set the wife about a bowl of broth for him, ordered him a cup of tea, bade him get up in the evenings, and promised to call again in a week when he would be well enough to show me all he had been doing with his farm. We walked five miles before getting home again, dodging here and there added so much to the distance.

Three more walks will I think finish my examination of those families connected with us, and perhaps introduce us to many much worse off and who, poor creatures, shall have all the help that we can give them after our own are served. We called in Blesinton on the Doctor, who is better but still in bed. The Colonel went up to see him and thinks him ill enough, quite overworked these wretched times; fever and dysentery among the people, distances so great, wet feet, fatigue, grief for the wretchedness that all our means can't overcome, most of it the consequence of the character of the sufferers who will be many generations yet before they rise to that higher perception of their duties which can alone ensure their greater comfort.

What would this country do without him? Where should we get such another friend and physician, devoting every energy to his professional duties? I have heart again now to relate my wanderings among the wretched, how wretched. Can strangers believe that a whole country would consider itself fed, on one good meal a day; could they manage a light supper besides for their children, three turnips and a pint of meal would quite content them for this latter purpose. Yet if all did as we do

– looked to their own – there would be no distress. But this system of public relief is an unjust mockery – nothing else.

* * *

Walk 3rd. [Actually the 4th.]

The distances being now greater I was able to take fewer houses on my round. I went up the hill again first calling on the Widow Quin, who being left some years ago on her husband's death insolvent, with a large and very young family and she an ailing woman, the Colonel relieved her of her land, forgave her seven years' rent, gave her the stock and crop to dispose of and left her the house and garden for her life. All her children were employed as they were fit for work and she has certainly done better than if she had retained her ill-managed farm. All her sons are in good places, one of them with us; her daughters married except one who lives with her and takes in washing. I put mother and daughter on the soup list, times being so hard. Two of the daughters are very well married; the third made a wretched one; she took a sickly labouring lad who is often laid up, but to whom she has brought seven children. They live in the mother's cowhouse where she had no right to put them and thus settle a whole family of beggars upon us, but we did not look after things then as we have learned to do now. It is the most wretched abode imaginable, without window or fire-place; mud for the floor, neither water nor weather-tight, nor scarce a door, all black with smoke, no furniture scarcely. Yet times are brightening for the nearly naked inmates. A brother in America sent them at Christmas ten pounds which paid their debts, and bought them some meal and fuel, and their eldest son is to go out to this kind uncle in March. They have no business where they are, the man not belonging to Baltiboys, but there they are, through our negligence, so we must take care of them for the present. I gave the poor woman a quarter's school fees for four of the children and put the family on the soup list, and when we come to the clothing which we must do for the very poor, she shall not be forgotten. Nothing could be cleaner or neater, in the rude way only known here, than the Widow Quin's comfortable three-roomed cabin.

The next visit was to a cousin Red Paddy Quin with a good farm which afford him every comfort from his good management; his wife lately died in childbed and her baby; he has two fine boys, the eldest at school, a little tidy girl as maidservant; two men, and plenty of everything. Little Paddy, a copy of Jack; with his boots, frieze great coat, and cap! and quite familiar with me from our school intercourse, and only seven years old, insisted on escorting me to the next house on the hill, the abode of another old pensioner, the plague of my life though I am very fond of her.

The widow Nary wants a few months of eighty, and there she was as brisk as a bee darning her stockings in the doorway without spectacles. As we provide her with everything in the world she wishes for, I merely called in to see how she was. She has found a decent little pedlar woman who was 'long in the army' to live with her, the only person she ever yet kept a second night with her, and the Colonel and I were so relieved at getting any one that pleased her, to look after her, that though this old campaigner has a son, we consented gladly thus to domicile them ... the son is a pet of mine, a dwarf, blind of one eye, marked deep with the smallpox, quite an object of ugliness, who working everywhere during the busy months, merely at boy's wages, always contrived to save enough for school during the winter. There he learned to net, by which trade he is now supporting his mother, her pedlar business being but sick now that every penny is required for food, as I know by my Repository at which we now sell nothing. Last year it nearly paid the expenses of the female school.

I came the back road home over the hill, down past the quarries and through the farm yards, looking in at the new room we have just contrived for the two men who sleep there to watch the cattle. I bought the furniture from Miss Gardiner, had it repaired and I don't believe any of the better farmers even possess as many comforts. We have eight bachelour labourers who all know they leave us if they marry. As they are, they are rich on their 6/- a week getting their soup or milk daily. Twelve out of door servants, four at 7/-; eight at 6/- makes a hole in small means, but this year we must keep them. Ten is our ordinary number. They are a truly decent set, grateful in earnest for their good places.

* * *

Walk the 4th. [Actually the 5th.]

Along this side of the hill, along the road behind the rockery, past the Darkers' excellent house where I did not call knowing well that all there was as one could wish. Northerns [Northerners], protestants, well educated, industrious, they are a credit to the country. Of the two brothers, John manages the good farm of ninety six acres; Tom is the Colonel's steward and bailiff at a salary of fifty pounds. Two maiden sisters take charge of the house, etc. Amongst them they have brought up five orphan nephews and nieces, the children of two brothers who died beggars.

Bartle Murphy's house on Baltiboys hill. While the family had few resources, Elizabeth described this house as 'very neat', and the family was 'better clothed than most.'

All that now remains of James Carney's 'good three roomed slated house'; he farmed 23 acres and had a 'pretty wife and four children'. (Séamas Ó Maitiú)

We have taken great pains with these children, indeed with the whole respectable family; lending them every book that was good for them and how their minds have grown – the women and all – prejudices and follies and affectations vanished, replacing gradually by good sound sense, without the odium of teaching either.

The next farm is in a bad way – a great annoyance to us, though owned by a most respectable woman the Widow Kelly. We have still a few of those miserable little patches of farms of 7 or 8 acres not having been able to get rid of all of them, so many subdivisions having been permitted during the negligent days of my brother-in-law and his careless agent; but this is the only farm we have [which is] not our own, which we can do nothing with for it is let on a lease of lives to a middleman, who sublets it to the Widow Kelly. She is a managing woman struggling on with twelve children on her sixty acres, very decently; but she is not improving her ground or her style of farming, or if she did we should not benefit, and she is letting the offices go to ruin. She has five children at school and plenty to feed all with; five acres of this leased ground are let to Bartle Murphy up at the top of the hill close by the moat which once defended one of Cromwell's watch towers. The colonel has planted all these furzy fields and Murphy has the charge of them at a small salary without which he must have been begging, the five acres having ruined him; his potatoes gone, his two cows dead of the murrain [a cattle disease], nothing left of all his labour but a cwt. and a half of oatmeal. There are six children, four at school, one at the breast, where, poor thing, it got nothing, a scanty breakfast and a turnip supper not providing much supply for it. All was very neat here and the clothes of the family of a better description than usual. The wife however broken hearted; it hardly raised her spirits to have her family put upon the soup list.

My last visit this day was to James Carny the mason; he is doing well on his farm of twenty three acres; has it well stocked, lives in a good three-roomed slated house with a pretty wife and four children, two of them at school; his trade hitherto kept him easy, but no one is building this year, so he has had to part with his men, his wife with her maid, to leave enough food behind.

* * *

After these extended visits to all the tenants on the estate, Elizabeth exclaimed that:

It's nonsense to talk of good landlords as the rule; they are no such thing, they are only the exception. In my walks about this little locality

> have I not found evidence against them that would fit me for a witness before a Committee of the House, on the causes of Irish misery? When I pass the limits of our own ground, nothing meets me but wretchedness. The other day when looking for a family we thought it our business to relieve, in the Weaver's Square where no looms are to be found now, every house I entered on my search broke my heart. The particular circumstances of this afflicting year have much encreased the misery, for the little farmers having no food to spare have dismissed their servants; the men leave their ground untilled, the women have eat their poultry, sold their pig, so do not want the help of a maid; thus young men and girls are returned upon their poverty-stricken parents, while between want of seed and want of hands to sow it, the prospects of a harvest are blighted; all rush to the roads which are rendered by this unprofitable labour impassable; there are two or three at hand actually shut up by the diggings and shovellings going on upon them and we are to pay for this waste, and for our ordinary and extraordinary expenses out of diminished funds. From Lord John's [the Prime Minister's] tone we hope they don't mean to tax the land with this misapplied million. If they do it will be very unjust. All exclaimed against the scheme, as useless in itself, preventing useful work and loosening the few remaining relations which yet attached the employed to the employer.

In the same month, George Cairns, one of the tenants, decided at last to emigrate to America. As mentioned by Elizabeth during her walk around the estate, Cairns seemed unable to work his holding, where there were 'fences broken, no gates, not a hoof on the land, not even a hen ...'. In addition, he owed two years' rent resulting in his land being taken from him. However, he was allowed to live on in his house pending his obtaining work as a sawyer, his trade or (as he eventually decided), emigrating. He had a wife and six children, and a cousin also lived with him who 'tried to prop him up'. When he made his decision to emigrate, he went about planning his departure:

> The poor man has gone up to Dublin to make his enquiries, carrying up a letter to John Robinson who will direct him and gather for our benefit all the information possible on the subject as probably others will follow this wise example. Old James Cullen is to give up his one acre and turn his attention to turf cutting, his married sons talk of America. Young James Doyle has gone; his uncle Barney Quin who is in a good place at Tulfarris talks of following him; his other uncles, mere day labourers, have no ambition as yet to better themselves but time, example, cold and hunger may teach them wisdom.

Eventually, Cairns fixed his departure date for 8 April, and Elizabeth's husband agreed to pay for the passage, but this was not the end of Cairns' problems:

> The poor man is unable to sell his furniture, little as he has of it, nobody has a penny to spare from food. The Colonel therefore buys it, and some old iron, and the manure. This will make a clothing and provision fund for him and he is to have five pounds as a present so that he may have something in hand on landing.

On the day of departure, the diary recorded that: 'Cairns is off today, begging to the last'. His cousin had decided to go with the family to America but Elizabeth and her husband refused to lend any money for his passage whereupon George Cairns himself came forward 'for the purpose'.

> ... seven pounds he produced from the secret drawer in his chest, and I have no doubt there is another seven pounds or more remaining, for he has paid no rent these two years, and in September he had forty pounds worth of hay, in January thirty-six barrels of oats, and with six with the cow would abundantly keep the family, more likely he won't land in America with only the Colonel's five pounds. Such a set – 'tis worth all they have cost to rid of them.

The reference, a few paragraphs back, to old James Cullen giving up his acre and turning his attention to turf cutting may cause today's reader to picture the old man having to struggle up the steep slopes of Moanbane mountain to dig his turf. In fact, this was not necessary as there were then extensive turf banks in the boggy ground which Elizabeth always referred to as the Bottoms – around the King's River close to Baltiboys, now lying far below the waters of the reservoir.

On several occasions, Elizabeth referred to various neighbouring landlords who made efforts to help their unfortunate tenants. She also repeatedly alluded to the misery suffered by the poor people then living not very far from Baltiboys under thoughtless and, in some cases, absentee landlords – especially around Hollywood and Dunlavin. Hollywood House, whose owner was an absentee landlord had been, like Tulfarris and Downshire House and, indeed, the Protestant churches of Ballymore Eustace and Hollywood, and the villages of Blessington and Dunlavin, victims of the 1798 Rising.

Elizabeth treated her servants in much the same manner as the tenants, and several references in her diary demonstrate how observant she could be of their various shortcomings. The following is a good example of this and shows that she was not unaware of her own shortcomings. She is writing about her housekeeper, Mrs Fyfe who, like Elizabeth, was Scottish:

> Two months too soon our coals are done, or nearer three, for thirty tons well managed are ample for the comfort of the house and always were sufficient till this year. Last June five ton remained in the cellar, thirty-one ton were added, and we brought with us from Dublin half a ton remaining over from our little store at the lodgings. As usual, Mrs Fyfe tells me 'We shall soon be out of coal ma'am', when she has one day's consumption in the house. Good, well meaning creature, no worse housekeeper ever tried the trade. I shall in future keep the key, give out what is proper, and if she don't like the plan she can leave us. Less than her wages would give us a good man servant, and the saving in coals, candles, sugar, would make up for other economies.

A day later she wrote the following postscript:

> The coal mishap has been quite a hurricane. I am rather mollified since the mighty lady admitted to the young ladies [Elizabeth's daughters] that she had been much to blame. It would have been both more respectful and wiser to have allowed this to her master and me. The organ of self-esteem must be preternaturally large in her otherwise diseased brain, for she is up like a sky rocket whenever she is found fault with or even interfered with. Quiet woman as I am, I emit the spark when much enforced, and she is, really, with all her valuable qualities, by no means an agreeable servant. I have much to put up with, my own easiness of temper being in fault originally. It don't do to be too yielding even in indifferent matters, particularly when there are arrogant or encroaching dispositions to deal with.

Neither Elizabeth nor her husband enjoyed robust good health, a fact which she commented upon at various times. Here she is writing about herself in March, 1847:

> I can't get well, so the doctor has me again and I think I shall get on after a while; that delicate stomach of mine is irritable to excess, the liver idle, bile abounding, no getting exercise, and the influenza hardly gone. What a slight hold have I of life; how small a matter would end my 'high imaginings', my hopes for these poor people, my anxieties for my children, my little 'world' of cares and duties, not always well attended to though always well intended.

Hal continued to suffer from asthma but on 29 March she noted that it was her husband's birthday and remarked on how well he now was. 'Better than we have seen him for years; so strong, able to walk for hours daily, to encounter winds that would kill me'. However, even if their health sometimes worried Elizabeth, they and the children walked quite a lot. As already noted, she usually walked when visiting tenants in fine weather. More than once she mentioned that the family had walked to church in Blessington and that she had walked to Russborough. The road to Blessington took the family past the ancient church and graveyard of Burgage. An early Christian site, it had a holy well and a number of inscribed stones. Its large early cross, known as St Mark's cross, was alluded to in Jane Pennington's account of her visit to Baltiboys quoted in the Introduction. The cross later fell down and was re-erected by members of the Stannus family, descendants of the Smiths at Baltiboys House. When the valley was flooded by the new reservoir in 1939, the cross and all the graves in the old burial ground were moved to higher ground further up Burgage Lane.

She also wrote of walking the 'dusty turnpike road' which linked Dublin, Blessington and Baltinglass. The turnpike trust to maintain this road was set up in 1829. It spent £1,581 in 1830 and £1,797 in 1831 on the 47 miles under its care. The trust ceased to exist under the Turnpike Abolition Act 1855. A fine example of a tollhouse still exists in Blessington and another has been turned into a public house further towards Baltinglass. On the roadside between Blessington and Baltinglass are still to be found a number of milestones dating from this time.

On one occasion she referred to the fact that she and the Colonel had walked to Rathbally, on the far side of Baltiboys Hill. 'We went this side the hill, up by Widow Mulligan's and up along the Common, round the Quaker graveyard and climbed the gate at Mr West's new entrance as we found it locked'. Scaling gates may not accord with most people's general notion of how nineteenth century landlords and their wives went around the countryside.

The month of April might have been expected to provide an improvement in the weather yet it was 'colder than in winter, ground white with snow both today and yesterday'. Added to this was the fact that the existing relief works were being wound down before the new ones were arranged so that there was virtually no work for the penniless peasantry.

On a more cheerful note, Elizabeth wrote that her Scottish Aunt Mary and a Mrs Bridges had each sent her five pounds to help in famine relief. 'Extreme kindness this, they are totally unconnected with Ireland and have already contributed to the general fund. We shall find this assistance truly seasonable for, truth to say, we were ourselves nearly run out'. Five pounds in the 1840s would be worth over £300 today.

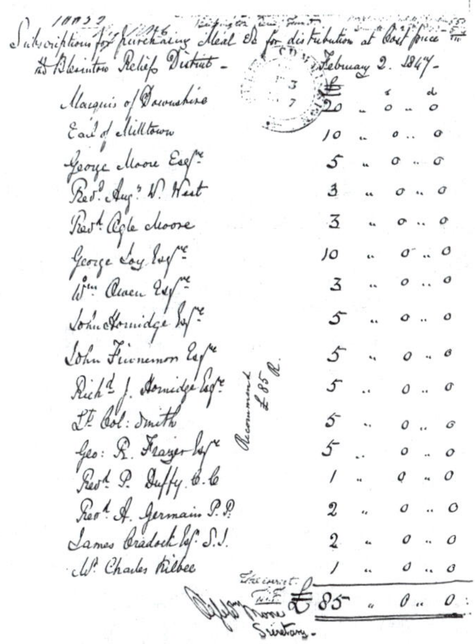
Subscriptions for purchasing Meal &c for distribution at Cost price in the Blesinton Relief District – February 2. 1847 –

	£	s	d
Marquis of Downshire	20	0	0
Earl of Milltown	10	0	0
George Moore Esqre	5	0	0
Revd. Augs W. West	3	0	0
Revd. Ogle Moore	3	0	0
George Hoy Esqre	10	0	0
Wm. Owen Esqre	3	0	0
John Hornidge Esqre	5	0	0
John Finnemore Esqre	5	0	0
Richd. J. Hornidge Esqre	5	0	0
Lt. Col: Smith	5	0	0
Geo: R. Frazer Esqre	5	0	0
Revd. P. Duffy C.C	1	0	0
Revd. A. Germain P.P.	2	0	0
James Cradock Esqr. S.J.	2	0	0
Mr. Charles Kilbee	1	0	0
	£85	0	0

Recommend £85 R.

The correct

Moore
Secretary.

'*Subscriptions for purchasing Meal, etc., for distribution at cost price in the Blesinton Relief District – February 2 1847.*'

A list of contributions from prominent members of the community around Blessington in February, 1847 is extant. The money was being collected to purchase meal to be sold at cost price. The Marquis of Downshire headed the list with a contribution of £20, followed by the Earl of Milltown with £15; Colonel Smith and most of the other landlords contributed £5 each, while Fr Germaine contributed £2. Elizabeth was critical of the Parish Priest of Black Ditches several times in relation to famine relief, so his contribution, something like £120 in today's money, demonstrates that, in the absence of corroborative evidence, Elizabeth's depiction of at least some events should be treated with caution.

It should also be noted that her views were being expressed on a day-by-day basis over a long period, so that it was reasonable for her opinions to alter with the changing circumstances. At times she regarded the government's handling of the famine crisis as nothing short of 'noble' while at other times she thought 'it is as if lunaticks were legislating'. Similarly, her opinion of the Irish character sometimes appeared equally contradictory, varying from despair at what she saw as dishonesty, excitability, lack of foresight, laziness, and even 'cuteness', on the one hand, to praising the people's quite remarkable morality. On one occasion, she described the Scots – her own race – as 'very far behind the maligned Irish', yet only a year or two earlier she had thought the Scots were a much calmer people, less given to violence and fighting. It was her view that the deficiencies in the Irish character were simply due to a lack of education; as she once expressed it: 'Is it not plain that properly educated they would be a fine and moral race'.

Around this time, unlike on an earlier occasion, she described Father Galvin, the curate of Black Ditches, as 'an enlightened young man, quite unalike any other priest we have hitherto had in these parts. Mr Galvin is a real blessing' adding, perhaps significantly, that 'he preaches upon the moral virtues, tries to instil good principles, praises England, the help it has given, the good it is aiming at ....' In April 1847, Elizabeth wrote that:

> ... the publick works hereabouts are over; the new act not yet in operation, distress therefore prevailing. As the two hills they were cutting [to make a new line of road], one at the schoolhouse, the other in Featherbed Lane, are unfinished, there is to be an application made to have them set on again which will employ the idle hands here for a week or two. So far we have come through very well; our district is favoured beyond other parts of this miserable country.

Elizabeth soon returned to the theme of public relief works with another comment about the money running out before the projected works could be completed, blaming it upon the way the men 'idled so shamelessly upon the roads'. Then, when the workers were dismissed, they went:

> ... in mobs to seek redress, got shillings here and there, and after five or six days the Committee met, struck a new rate, presented for the completion of the works, sent their minutes up to Dublin where the Board [of Works] will forward them to the Treasury which will consider them, pass them, return them; then an advance of money will be asked for, granted, and the labour will begin again; no day, however, yet fixed and twelve have already passed since all means of earning a subsistence have been denied to our paupers.

All of this seems to represent a good description of officialdom in action, or perhaps inaction.

* * *

Relief works took various forms, one of which was land drainage. It was Elizabeth who, as early as 1842, proposed the notion of embarking on a

Elizabeth had her name carved in granite when she built Lacken school in 1869, after inheriting money from an aunt. (Séamas Ó Maitiú)

comprehensive drainage scheme at Baltiboys. She had commented at that time that she was reading-up on the subject, especially about a new method perfected by a Mr Smith of Deanston in Scotland. She wrote: 'I mean to drain and to improve the property of Baltiboys, if I live a few years we shall see whether I do it. Hal laughs, so he always does...'

Four years later, the said Hal, instead of laughing, was considering borrowing 'some few hundreds from the Government and draining the whole of his property, the terms are very advantageous for the borrower, 3½%, repaid by instalments in twenty years'. But Elizabeth's husband was cautious, carefully reading:

> the Labour Act, the Drainage Act, and the Secretary's letter, all having to be rightly understood and reconciled if possible with the orders of the Board of Works, none of them seeming to our plain capacities to run well together.

The idea of improving the land and at the same time giving employment to the local poor was especially attractive to Elizabeth. In April 1847, the Baltiboys agent went to the Board's offices in Dublin:

> ... to acquaint himself properly with drainage proceedings ... We think it will cost about a thousand pounds to drain this side of the hill alone but we have twenty-two years to pay it in, by yearly instalments of six and a half per cent and, as after the second year there must be a profit upon the work of ten per cent and there may be one of twenty or

> upwards, the speculation is good. It will give a deal of employment and so lighten the rates.

The surveyor under the Drainage Commissioners verified the Colonel's survey of the lands to be drained and the amount of the loan was £1,200. Two months later, Elizabeth expressed the hope that 'we shall soon have a band of poor men at work'. It was not until October that the Colonel received the first order on the Treasurer of the Board of Works for the drainage works and even a week after this the work had not begun, because some necessary plans were not yet executed. 'Was there ever such an office for delays?' wrote an exasperated Elizabeth. When the plans arrived they were accompanied by 'a very long account of the various soils upon that part of the property' and Elizabeth fretted about the continuing procrastination but more especially over the loss of the two months which had been, as she put it, 'best suited for the purpose'. There was, apparently, a sinister side to all this: 'It seems that there are large sums missing, one of the under officers of the Board is lodged in jail on suspicion of having embezzled for his share about eight thousand pounds'.

Tom Darker, the Baltiboys steward, supervised the works when, at last, they got started:

> He divided his men into five gangs, six men to a gang, so that their work is easily supervised, changed, or their numbers added to, he thinks another gang will include all the unemployed, the Colonel being resolute to take no discharged servants. They, the farmers, are beginning the same tricks they played with the public works last year, relieving themselves of their labourers – of course to the detriment of their farms, penny wise and pound foolish ... There is no such thing as truth or honour or conscience in this country – high or low – speaking generally.

The drainage works continued into the new year when Elizabeth wrote:

> Our out o' door works are progressing. Richard Hornidge has begun draining with his own money, so employs another good band of men, still, numbers are idle and the Doctor tells us that influenza and fever are so general as to produce much distress.

In May, the drainage operations at Baltiboys encountered a new problem when Bryan Dempsey, one of the tenant farmers, refused to allow his farm to be drained and even refused to allow his landlord's carts to cross his fields to drain other farms. The Agent tried to reason with Dempsey who 'threatened violence, spoke most impudently ... vowed he did not care ...

he laid a sovereign that no man should dig a sod on his ground but himself'. Dempsey prevented access for a second time on the following day so the carts were employed in drawing stones from the quarry until such time as a magistrate was consulted.

> Whatever may be advised for the present, my own opinion is that the Colonel will take the opportunity of serving a notice to quit upon this troublesome man, now that the feeling will be universal against him. He would be a good riddance for his character is detestable and I believe detested. But he is dangerous, for though too great a coward to commit murder himself he would hire an assassin as soon as he would a labourer ... I can't make out what Dempsey wants or means. He would be benefited by this draining like the rest of the Tenants, his land improved, himself and son and servants and horses employed, and any little mischief caused by cart tracks, etc. would be paid for; it seems like a fit of frenzy.

The matter ended a week or two later when Dempsey, 'finding the law was against him ... he submitted, ungraciously enough, announcing to his neighbours that having vindicated his rights, he [had] permitted matters to proceed'. In the autumn, the Smiths sent cattle to the fairs at Naas and Rathsallagh but 'all came home as before'. A few weeks afterwards, Elizabeth wrote that the:

> ... cattle dealers in Dublin have gone and caused immense distress, in fact paralysed the markets; not an offer for a beast of any sort at any of the late fairs. Banks, merchants, agents, all are bankrupt in all places. John Robinson [their agent] has lost seven thousand pounds by bad debts, trusting people who have failed to pay ... people are oppressed by this frightful amount of bankruptcies, almost everyone, either themselves or their friends affected by some of these numerous failures ... then the winter prospects look very gloomy. The destitution is expected to be wider spread than last year, for the very poor will be very nearly as ill off while the classes above, which then relieved them, are all this year in serious difficulties. No money anywhere, the little hordes of cash and goods all spent and nothing to replace either. The ministry says the land must support the people on it. Half the country having been left untilled for want of means to carry it out while a mint of money was squandered in destroying the roads, much of it finding its way into the pockets full enough before.

When the 1847 Public Relief Works ended at harvest time, she commented that:

10 Vict., Cap. 32.

DUPLICATE.

ORDER FOR A LOAN.

To
Henry Smith
Esqre.

£1,200

Sec. of Public Works

By Authority—Alex. Thom, 87, Abbey-street, Dublin.

The within named William Boswell Hogan of Woodville Sandford in the County of Dublin, Solicitor Maketh Oath and saith, that he is a subscribing Witness to the Order of which the within writing is a Duplicate, and also to the within Duplicate Order; and saith that he saw the Seal of the Commissioners of Public Works in Ireland duly affixed to said Order and Duplicate; and saith the name W.B. Hogan ———— subscribed as a Witness to the Execution of said Order and Duplicate, is this Deponent's proper name and handwriting, and saith he delivered said Order and Duplicate to John E Chapman Esq., Assistant Register, at the Registry Office, King's Inns, in the City of Dublin, at the hour of ~~minutes~~ one o'Clock in the after noon of Monday the Eighteenth day of October instant.

W.B. Hogan

Sworn before me this 18th day of October 1847,
at the Registry Office, King's Inns, City of Dublin.

John E Chapman

The order for a loan of £1,200, obtained by Colonel Smith in October 1847 when he embarked on a comprehensive drainage scheme for his estate.

> ... few have been receiving assistance of late, comparatively, there being plenty of work for those who choose to go to look for it. The class who can't earn is no larger than it ever was, it is now thrown upon the Poor Law guardians, who at their meeting on Friday last, instead of electing relieving officers to take charge of the several districts, as they were called together to do, fell into disputing about a set of jobs they had a mind to perpetrate. They wanted to join large districts and lump the pay, thus making a good income for a *son* or *nephew* who would have been physically incapable of getting through such an extent of duties. ... The seventeen divisions of our union are to be paired, two and two, the *three* smallest only going at the end together, and Mr Owen [Lord Downshire's agent] had the address to join Blesinton and Baltiboys, so we shall get on comfortably, for with our many ordinary works and our extraordinary draining and our better description of landlords. We are by no means *swamped* with paupers, even though part of the mountains, Shannon Harbour and Weavers Square are included [in the Blessington and Baltiboys district]. Land property must be sold in these miserable parts of the country, where the landlords have been keeping up false appearances, living like wealthy men while drowned in debt. And the equally improvident tradesman must publish his insolvency, break and lie and cheat no more. The whole people, so to speak, have been existing on credit, make believe, there was nothing real about far more than half of them.

* * *

Despite all the problems encountered during the year, Elizabeth's journal entry for 31 December reads:

> ... the last day of the year – the happy year 1847 I may call it – so far no serious affliction has occurred in the family. Many arrangements for good have been made among us, and the poor people particularly depending on our ownselves have come through these troubled times so far without much suffering. Better hopes seem rising for future years – the famine having roused the energies of this clever race. Nothing else I believe would have spirited them up to the exertion indispensable to their decent comfort.
>
> In all Baltiboys we have no destitute family; a very few distressed. Dick Gray who from drinking, gambling, company-keeping and children reared amid these vices, is the most so and we will not help him for he will not give up his land nor till it properly, nor live reputably, yet he has done wonders for him this summer. Mick and Judy Doyle are more

> omfortable looking than really in want; they owe nothing and as they e by hard labour made a good deal of money, their dirty sloppy ways e their own choice. The old Byrnes are poor enough; they went on e old system and, having spent in their youth, have nothing in their age but the labour of their son Luke, he has four mouths besides his own to provide for. Clothes must be out of his power. Pat Quin is not so deserving of assistance because there are other brothers and sisters able to assist him to support his mother. One sister is indeed an object – the blind woman married to the lame Jem Doyle. They had no business to marry, no right to squat themselves down in that cow house, but there they are and God help them. I have not forgot them this Christmas. They and the old Byrnes must be looked after. Mary Ryan having left the Poor House I am done with her. She is sharing the misery of the grandmother – another mouth for the lame uncle to fill, and so be it; they must take their own way, reason is lost on them.

In one more comment on the extensive draining scheme completed earlier in the year, Elizabeth wrote this brief reference: 'The drainage being over, the same distress exists as before it began.' By this she meant, not that the draining was a failure but that the employment given by the scheme had stopped. Elizabeth added: 'we have kept the people in our immediate neighbourhood alive these two years and now they must die, or beg, or steal, any thing rather than the Poor House . . .'

1848

"We in Baltiboys must descend a few pegs"

At the end of January, 1848, the diaries record that there was 'six inches of snow lying evenly over the country. Except that it stops the outwork we ought to be glad to see it to keep the ground warm, to purify the air, and drive fever away' Elizabeth Smith quickly returned to the subject of the 1847 drainage works when, one Sunday, her husband brought a young Mr Dennis home with him from church. He was a well-connected man, the son of an old Mr Dennis [of Fort Granite House near Baltinglass], nephew to the Saunders [of Saunders' Grove near Baltinglass] cousin to Mr Tynte [of Tynte Park near Dunlavin], and Lord Aldboro, [of Stratford Lodge, also near Baltinglass]. This young Mr Dennis had just succeeded as surveyor under the Drainage Commissioners, taking the place of a Mr Sullivan 'who has been taken off by typhus fever, with 100 more, 1,000 more!' This item of news, coupled with so much else that was amiss, was followed by a somewhat melancholy entry:

> Begging is becoming general again. The markets are falling, corn 8/6 and will be lower. Rents indeed, shall we live, my God what a spring we have before us. I hope I am in a gloomy mood and see terrours where there are only difficulties. Yet everyone who thinks wears a long face.
>
> A report that the income tax is to be raised to five per cent, Ireland included. For a wise purpose we might bear this better, but if the reason of such an additional burthen upon those nearly ruined already be to add to our already too large military force, this miserable ministry should be turned adrift. All rational persons should join with all their power to prevent such a cruel encrease to our difficulties. I don't see how we in Ireland can meet it. We in Baltiboys must descend a few more pegs. Governess, carriage, hunters are gone already. Butler and house-keeper must follow. These luxuries can be done without, and after a while we shall hardly miss them, only it frets one to feel that we give up our comforts for a political folly.

While there were various references to the general shortage of money, one quoted incident appeared to contradict this. The Smiths attended an auction at Kilbride Manor and were somewhat surprised to see many local small farmers purchasing, resulting in Elizabeth's comment: 'Does it not seem as if there were no lack of money among [that] class generally. All is paid for before being carried away; there was no lack of thirty shilling notes, which have not been current these two years as they are no longer issued'

Not long after this, on a visit to the Finnamore family at Ballyward, the Smiths were told the story of a tenant who owed a neighbour, Mr Hornidge, several years rent. The tenant held only a few acres and he came:

> ... with the usual apology and the usual excuses, large family, bad times, sickness, etc. He had three pounds to give on *account* which no way lightened the arrears, but he had done his best. Fumbling into his pocket he produced three notes which, on Mr Hornidge examining them, proved to be three ten pound notes. He took them gravely, pulled out his books, made out the man's accounts clear and, handing him a small balance, informed him of his mistake, and that he did not now owe him a penny.

In yet another reference to the fact that her family was not wealthy, Elizabeth wrote: 'Everything is cheap enough were there money to buy with. But nowhere is there any'. And again: ' I can't pay poor Miss Clerk her half years' salary. I have given her five pounds to account merely. The Colonel spends nothing: he sold his horse to help us, gave up the Deccan prize money he had intended to build a lodge with, and I have put off paying the girls [her daughters] the money borrowed from them last year'. Short of money or not, Elizabeth also was able to count her blessings and painted this little portrait of their family life:

> I often think, when the Colonel is sleeping over the Newspaper in his easy chair, and I look around the prettily furnished drawing-room, with its comforts, its bright hearth, the lamp upon the little table, the children all engaged in different ways, those children who have not yet given one serious uneasiness, that in this world wide, a happier family could not well be found. What are the troubles of our quiet lot, for when there is such a fund to draw on for support under them. Being prudent, we have felt the money difficulties of these bankrupt years much less than most others. We have been able to help our poor neighbours to a greater extent in consequence, no small comfort, and if times don't mend we can cheerfully bring our habits down to meet

> them, conscious that no one suffers loss by or through us. I wonder dear children, will you smile over our family history when you come to read this record of bygone days.

At the end of May, Elizabeth mentioned that the family drove 'to Cuylbeg, a private picnic, so very pleasant'. This was, in fact, Kylebeg Lodge (Kilbeg on modern O.S. maps), about a mile south-east of Lacken, the shooting lodge owned by Tom Sheehan, a friend of the Smith family, who was the editor of the Dublin *Evening Mail.* She described the Lodge as very comfortable, that they dined 'in his only hall, out of which, all round, open the small batchelour bedrooms. A good kitchen behind, attentive servants'.

* * *

The year 1848 has been called 'the Springtime of the Nations', a time when many parts of Europe witnessed uprisings – including Austria, the Czech lands, France, Germany, Hungary, Italy, Poland and, of course, Ireland. Smith O'Brien insisted that in 1848, revolution was more justified in Ireland than in any other European country but, one way or another, they all ended in failure, not least the latter which ended almost as soon as it had begun. The 1848 uprising lacked any pretence of the element of surprise; it was badly organised and was so badly timed (a few weeks before the harvest during one of the worst years of the famine) that it never had any real chance of success.

William Smith O'Brien was a prosperous man, educated in England, and is said to have spoken like an Englishman. Elizabeth must have found it difficult to understand how a man of his wealth, an MP, a landlord, *and* a Protestant, (who claimed to trace his roots back to Brian Boru), could have allied himself to such a hopeless cause. Whatever chance the rising might have had was frittered away with marching and counter-marching, mostly around County Tipperary. No doubt this was why Elizabeth made several references in her journal to what she called 'the Tipperary Boys'. The insurgents, in their first major encounter, surrounded a force of policemen in a house near Ballingarry and after a half-hearted attack and the arrival of more police, the engagement was called off and the leaders went into hiding. Not surprisingly, O'Brien later wrote that it had been a fatal miscalculation and said that it did not deserve the name of 'insurrection'. After his capture he was tried for high treason, found guilty and sentenced to death with a recommendation for mercy. He refused to apply for a pardon – the only means by which he could be reprieved – and a special Act of Parliament was passed enabling the government to transport him to

Tasmania. Pardon came six years later and he returned home in 1856. All this is the background to a series of journal entries about 'the physical force section' during the spring and summer of that year and to a number of expressions of concern that political agitation further south might spread to County Wicklow. The following quotation gives a fair idea of how Elizabeth saw these activities

> The physical force section make no way, that is certain and therefore I am sorry the three truly contemptible leaders [William Smith O'Brien, Thomas Meagher and John Mitchell] have been indicted for their seditious speeches at their Hall where they figure away once a week of an evening, supported by a newspaper [the *United Irishman*], the most impudent that ever attempted to disturb a nation. They were held to bail and then returned to their vocation to preach 'down with the Queen, a republic for ever! fraternity with France', and every conceivable folly. They must be cracked...

A few weeks after this, in April 1848, Elizabeth wrote:

> Dublin [is] all military, and only just in time, for the pike-making was going on by night and by day, muskets arriving from Birmingham, even small brass cannon, and the rifle practice was regular in many towns ... The Lord Lieutenant's determination has over-awed the agitators, the unexpected answer given by the French to their ridiculous deputation has quite depressed them, in fact the rebellion has evaporated.

Elizabeth had this to say after the French turned down Smith O'Brien's request for assistance:

> The Government deserves the utmost credit for the vigour with which they have met this first open attempt at rebellion ... All this has quieted Ireland. Every precaution is taken to prevent mischief til the new law be passed, when the authorities will be enabled to deal so summarily with these audatious broilers that they will soon retire either to Botany Bay or obscurity.

Later, after reading about all the unrest in Europe, Elizabeth returned to the subject of what she termed 'our State trials':

> Mr Meagher was acquitted by one dissentist Juryman. Mr Smith by two ... Mr Mitchell was found guilty, sentenced to fourteen years transportation, carried from the dock to the steamer which immediately

> set sail, and he has left his native land for ever...

The brief uprising actually took place in August when Elizabeth was in Scotland on a family visit. When she read about it in the newspapers there, she commented: 'What do you think of the rebellion now? ... Poor Smith O'Brien must be mad. I see Wicklow is proclaimed'. Writing to Hal at Baltiboys, she advised:

> If there is likely to be any disturbance near our hills you had really better come away. I don't fear it myself, still I am sure Redmond, Dempsey and some others [tenants in Baltiboys] are up to any mischief, though perhaps too cowardly to aid a failing, we may say a fallen, cause. The manner in which the Government has pounced on their prey, just in the very nick of time, is worthy of all praise.... Poor Smith O'Brien ... routed by fifty police. It is very creditable to that body, requiring no military aid. Really the times are very exciting at home and abroad.

* * *

In September, the Smiths received an invitation to a *dejeuner* from an acquaintance, Mr Armstrong, who lived at Kippure Park, on the road from Kilbride to the Sally Gap. The invitation was to witness the laying of the foundation stone of a new bridge, at Ballysmuttan, over the river Liffey 'near a dangerous ford where many people have been drowned.' (The date, 1848, may still be seen at the base of one of the pillars). Elizabeth wavered about going but eventually decided that if she refused, none of the rest of the family would go either. Somewhat reluctantly, she went and this is her description of the outing:

> Well! we really had a day of it, forty people besides *mob* assembled at the ford. Lady Downshire laid the stone, presented with a silver trowel on a silk cushion by Mr Armstrong; hurrahs quite deafening, then four horns played *God save the Queen* then Mr Armstrong read a speech, more hurrahs. Lord Downshire replied. Horns played *See the conquering Hero*. Ten gentlemen were then presented with red and blue cockades, thus constituted Stewards, to keep order. Then all the carriages drove to Kippure [Park]. The horns played the March in *Figaro* and *Away on the mountain's brow*. Sheep well bellied met us on the lawn. Arrived at the door, horns played *Home sweet home*. A longish interval of conversation, then the banquet, very well got up indeed, hot and cold, stout and sweet, fruit, flowers and champaign. My Lord handed me to

> the left of our host, my lady being on his right. We had a good song, retired to the drawing room, several good songs, coffee, tea, and then adjourned to the Barn where all, high and low, mixed in the *Social dances*, as it will be put in the newspapers, where we expect to see a flaming paragraph composed by Mr Armstrong himself; he always puts himself and his doings in the papers.

'My Lord' was the Fourth Marquis of Downshire; his father had died in 1845 while the Smiths were in France. He died of 'apoplexy' while out riding near Blessington and the event must have caused quite a stir in the area. The new, young lord was much better liked by Elizabeth, his obvious delight mixing with the landlords of the Blessington area being highly appreciated.

After these jollifications, Elizabeth once more became gloomy about the prospects ahead:

> We are to have a hard winter and no fuel in the country; so much rain during the summer prevented any turf being dried or much being cut. The people are also beginning to look very ragged, they have bought no new clothes since the potatoes failed, all their scanty earnings being required for food; the children are half naked. We must do something for those who come to school – it is pitiable to see them.

In November she wrote that the weather was continuing 'impropitious' with very cold winds and the ground too wet for ploughing:

> ... yet there is hardly any sickness in the country, even among the poor, a singular thing at this season with little food and no fire. Driving about, the many unroofed cabins give additional desolation to the wet and dirty lanes. The moment the Poor House receives its inmates the wretched dwelling is destroyed so that a return is impossible. Quantities are still, even at this season, going off to America, many of them with plenty of money in their pockets! And we miss them not. The winter will surely make some room.

Although she was also gloomy about the prospects for her own class, Elizabeth remained confident that her family would survive by continuing to adopt a more modest style of living:

> It is the intention of the Government to root out the present proprietors of the soil *en masse*. They wish to finish them; perhaps they are not wrong, for as a class they have failed altogether to do their duty, but

why crush the few righteous with the many erring? The English capitalists are waiting till the glut in the market still further reduces the value of land; it can now be had for fifteen or sixteen years' purchase; they expect it to fall to twelve. This will annihilate our present aristocracy. Those of us who can struggle through will, in time, rise from the ashes fresh and vigorous, but how few there will be and how much must we first suffer. I think Mr Moore is more dispirited than need be because his own affairs are in such a desperate condition. Still we must all prepare to look the evil in the face, that penury may not overtake us unawares. We have no debts to speak of. We have a fair stock and horses sufficient to cultivate more land than we now have in our own hands, and three hundred a year [pension] good from the E.I. [East India] Company, so that I cannot see want before us. A reduced style of living may be requisite and what the worse shall we be of that? Many parts of the country are quite deserted – inhabitants all emigrated or in the Poor Houses none left to till the ground and the landlords totally ruined are without capital to manage it themselves; without skill either maybe, or energy or will or all together. Certainly nothing of all this is to be seen here. I cannot help thinking there is much exaggeration in these reports.

Elizabeth had mentioned in that last entry that they had 'horses sufficient to cultivate more land than we have in our hands' yet, only a couple of months earlier she had written in her journal that:

Burgage is in the market, and he [her husband] seems to me to have very much set his heart upon purchasing it. We have tabled over the scheme, and to me it seems a bad one, but I have no business head. Had we the money ready it might do all very well, but to borrow the money leaves a very small profit out of rents not altogether secure while a large head rent must be always ready. He will, I hope, consult a lawyer before thus encumbering himself with what may prove an annoyance. At our age we want repose. Work and speculations are for the young.

Conditions varied very considerably from county to county as is well known but that there were quite stark differences even in adjoining districts is already clear from Elizabeth's often repeated descriptions of the contrast between the area around Baltiboys and the position of the poor in neighbouring Hollywood, Dunlavin and Baltinglass, and also to the west around Naas. A Scottish cousin who had just returned from a tour of the south of Ireland told Elizabeth that 'the perfection of a few isolated spots where good landlords had created a little paradise contrasted painfully with the desolation of the scenes *en masse*'. A friend brought first-hand news from County Kilkenny where, he reported, the gentry was 'all cleared out, farmers to America with several years rents in their pockets; peasantry unemployed and ripe for anything', by which he meant conditions were so extreme that some people were prepared to commit themselves to any action from stealing or murder to open rebellion. One man, a mill owner, 'never walks unattended and both he and his companions carry their pistols in their hands ready locked'.

* * *

Elizabeth was greatly relieved when she heard it was being proposed that the Poor Law Commissioners were going to rearrange the local districts so that Baltinglass and Naas would no longer be part of the same district as Lower Talbotstown, where Baltiboys was situated. An official report had described Baltinglass as a "nucleus for misery" so the proposed new arrangement would provide, as Elizabeth expressed it:

> a charming union. All interconnected, all lying together, no part too distant to be superintended, and no great amount of pauperism in the district ... We have spent much time and much money and much energy in faithfully doing our duty among our own people, all of us, and it is certainly only fair to let us benefit by it; it was very unfair to swamp us with the neglected districts of our neighbours.

An entry in Elizabeth's journal in the closing weeks of 1848 confirms that the Baltiboys estate had continued to fare reasonably well during the year:

> By a statement the Colonel and I made out, we get of profit from our landed property but one hundred and twenty pounds; last year, owing to backward rents, but forty eight. This however clears all outlay even to workmen's and outside servants' wages, leaving us our farm of one hundred and twenty acres to support the house-hold, the stable and the stock, and then we have three hundred and twenty clear, of pay, besides the occasional sale of a horse and my scribblings. As John Robinson says, who is so well off in these times; he feels sure there is not such another well to do property in Ireland; it is very small and we live on it.

On the last day of the year, she wrote:

The end of 1848. Were I in a moralising mood what a pamphlet would I write of all the deeds and doings and feelings and changes of this most eventful year. But I am indisposed for any mental exertion – overcome probably by the weight of materials, for there never were more teeming times.

The testimonial fountain, which was erected in Blessington 'as a tribute of respect from the tenantry to the third Marquis of Downshire', stands in front of the old Market House. (Dermot James)

The farm bell at Baltiboys House which was not rung when Ninette de Valois was born because she was not the expected son and heir. She was a great-great granddaughter of Elizabeth Smith. (Dermot James)

1849

"God help the country, man won't, seemingly"

The new year saw Elizabeth Smith again preoccupied with the state of the family's finances – hardly surprising when she was acutely aware that many landlords were heavily in debt and some were facing bankruptcy:

> The upper classes are now suffering, the farmer class a good deal, the landlord class a great deal. Every day we hear of the ruin of additional families, of course among those who had been improvident, either themselves or their ancestors, yet who managed to live and let live till these unjust poor laws came to overwhelm them. That we have so far escaped is owing entirely to the Honourable East India Company's pay, [the Colonel's pension] small though it be, for the little property having but a debt of £1,000 upon it would yield but a bare £100 a year for the support of its owner after all the charges on it were paid, unless we were to dismiss all the servants and labourers. We are tight enough as it is and must try and lessen our expenditure still. One labourer the Colonel has dismissed, and he has only a helper in the stables at labourer's wages, Pat having accepted the reduced situation till the 1st March when he goes into the police. We shall also try and sell another young horse, their keep is very costly....
>
> We are living now upon that £15, [payment for a magazine article] not another penny in the house can there be till the pay comes in February. I had to refuse Mr Darker any help to pay his wages yesterday, he must learn to feel that his farm employs too many, the labour on it and his own salary quite absorb the profits, that and the stable, it is not the house, yet the house I would willingly remodel and now that I am stronger, take any amount of trouble myself, provided suitable retrenchments are carried through in other departments. A woman's candle-end savings are worth little and they frequently destroy all family comfort. It is the luxuries that tell in every way, one of these dispensed with renovates the domestick system. Upper servants, fancied wants, indolent habits, can all be dispensed with and no real happiness sacrificed,

but there must be two to the bargain.

She went on to forecast a social revolution and hoped for an 'infusion of healthy democracy':

> What are the Lords but feudal Barons? What are the Commons but their kith and kin? What are the Army and the Navy in their extravagant extent and most costly arrangement but provisions for their Cadets? What are the Colonies but refuges for their castaways, the church but an opprobrium on our Christian profession? And for all these idle supercilious ignoramus's the working publick is taxed, heavily taxed, not in their superfluities, in their luxuries, but in the very necessaries of life. Matters cannot go on thus. There is too much power in the middle classes, the real strength of the state, to endure longer such misgovernment.

A week after this she was to add this wry comment: 'Wouldn't I govern this state, and can't govern my own household! We are fools all'.

Snippets of news from London sometimes resulted in terse comments from Elizabeth: 'Such a Queen's speech as this day has reached our Irish eyes has surely never been exceeded for folly by any of the long line of insipid predecessors'. She then went on: 'the two houses of Parliament have appointed committees to enquire into the Poor Laws, heaven knows what they will make of it, nothing till too late most likely'; and then: 'a grant of fifty thousand to feed the West of Ireland, which it is calculated will last a month or barely'. In February, Elizabeth wrote the following sardonic comment on a proposed new 'rate in aid' whereby the wealthier areas of the country were expected to contribute to the poor:

> ... a new rate in aid, but only of sixpence, as thus – An electoral division, when rated beyond five shillings can apply for aid to the Union, when the Union is taxed beyond seven and sixpence it applies to something else, when that reaches nine and sixpence, the country at large is taxed the sixpence. Beyond this ten shillings, compulsory aid will not go, but it certainly soon will reach it. And the remaining ten shillings has to pay rent, rent charge, head rent, tithes, cess, dispensaries, charities, and support the family. It is as if lunaticks were legislating.

'We were truly astonished', Elizabeth wrote a fortnight later, 'by the door opening and Lord Downshire entering, the Doctor for his companion.' She continued:

> He has run over on an agitating mission to try to get up petitions against this odious rate in aid. He won't have much trouble, there is quite a fury against it, such determined resolutions as makes one tremble for the consequences. Such an unjust proposal. When a property can't pay its rates and other burdens why not sell it. Why keep its pauper possessor and all depending on him hanging on in a state of misery and then insist on industrious neighbours supporting all these beggars. The rate itself is so small it is hardly worth noticing as a grievance if it were fair to levy it, or if it would do permanent good, or even prevent misery; but nothing of the kind, the principle is faulty, tend to level all property, destroy all energy and finally involve us all in ruin. Lord John [Russell, the Prime Minister] wishes to carry it out at once before hearing evidence but was out voted, and his opinions afterwards much modified by the examination of two of the poor law commissioners. This is our Prime Minister, this is legislation. God help the country, man won't seemingly .... Hereabouts they may refuse to pay it, but they will let it be levied; police, or at any rate military will collect it easily. In the north [where farmers had threatened not to pay the rate] what they say, that will they do, and bloodshed may follow.

Some time later, with a sense of relief, Elizabeth was able to write that 'the Committee in the Lords have thrown out the rate in aid, a majority of thirteen to seven condemn it as impolitick, insufficient, unjust, and without a precedent; exactly the truth'. She then continued:

> ... they little know the truth in England. So ill-used a people as the Irish don't exist, and those poor laws have completed the ruin of us. That little fool, [her description of Russell], whose head really seems of late to have left him. Not one single remedial measure can that shallow brain propound .... Charity on compulsion given by the industrious to the idle is all this wretched substitute for a statesman can think of as a way of scrambling through another season of hunger, disease and death.

There was more to Elizabeth's sarcasm about the Prime Minister than, perhaps, meets the eye. Two decades earlier, after serving for two terms as MP for Tavistock, her own father was compelled to stand-down by Russell's father who wanted the seat for Lord John's step-brother. When this happened, her father was already weighed-down by his ruinous financial problems and this was to prove the last straw, forcing him to leave the country for India – later bringing his family there too – and he never again saw the old highland estate of which he had once been the proud Laird.

Two fairs held during the month of April reflected the general state of things: 'Fair as well as market at Blesinton, plenty of sellers but no buyers. Ewes and lambs from twelve to sixteen shillings each pair, a fat bullock six pounds'. A week later 'a bad fair at Naas, none of our cattle sold, nor did much stock change hands. The weather is such that no grazier would think of buying and really I don't believe there is money in the country. The respectable emigrants have carried away, it is said, about three millions which used to be floating agricultural capital'. A week after this she wrote that:

> Tom Quin, the carrier, is almost ruined by having advanced money for the little shopkeepers up and down the country as was his custom, and he cannot get repaid. He spent a day going from one to the other and out of fifty three pounds due, he received seven [shillings] and sixpence

Up to this time, with only a few exceptions, most of the Baltiboys tenants had managed to pay their rents but on the last day in May 1849, when rents were once again due, Elizabeth recorded it had been:

> ... a very bad rent day, little money going, some of those that should have paid did not pay, others who were hard enough pushed brought what they could, more is promised shortly, but it is a chance whether the poor creatures will be able to avoid encreasing their November arrears.

That the famine affected not only the poor but also the middle classes and the rich – albeit very differently – is made clear time and again in Elizabeth's journal. Lord Milltown and his family who lived, as Elizabeth expressed it, 'in that cathedral of a house' [her description of Russborough] were facing bankruptcy due to a combination of the knock-on effects of the famine and his lordship's propensity for gambling. Calling to visit 'Milady', as Elizabeth sometimes called the Countess, the journal records that the Milltowns were:

> ... penniless, their creditors have begun to lose patience, they are without a hope, I never felt so much almost for anyone. Who can reckon faults when there is so much distress. She brought such a fortune and now to be reduced so low. She has no funds, no energy, no fortitude, no occupation, no temper. What a subject for such heavy misfortunes. Her Lord was keeping her too low, and he can't sooth her, and really very little would make her a lunatick, there is the beginning undoubtedly. She gossiped herself into better spirits, laughed as of old and ate two peaches and broiled chicken while we talked, which did her a deal of

The former fever hospital in Blessington, now a private house. Established in 1849, Colonel Smith and others subscribed to a fund to provide a nurse, provisions and fuel. (Séamas Ó Maitiú)

Most of the old Poor Houses have been either demolished or greatly altered. This photograph shows a recently restored Poor House at Dunshaughlin. (Dermot James)

good. I promised to go back today, but it looks too rainy.

One of the consequences of the financial problems facing Lord Milltown was an auction of horses, mares and foals at Russborough where, a few days later, a total of twenty-two were on offer:

> Each one was brought out by its own attending groom and paraded before a very small crowd of buyers, it was a parade indeed for his actual stable servants are reduced to eight, the rest were the labourers, white jacketed for the occasion. There was no bidding, a colt was sold to O'Connor Henchy for thirty pounds, a filly to Mr King for fifteen, a brood mare with her foal to a dealer for forty pounds, and considering the times these were fair prices, for the description of horses was not very saleable and half of them were foundered [lame] or spavined [swollen hocks] or aged.

The above-named O'Connor Henchy lived at Stonebrook, near Ballymore Eustace. He became an MP in 1852 and High Sheriff for County Kildare in 1884. James King, also named, lived at Humphrystown and his son, another James, was later to marry Elizabeth's daughter Annie.

Besides the Milltowns, a second local family facing financial ruin was that of the Reverend William Ogle Moore, Rector of Blessington and Kilbride. According to Elizabeth, his problems were the result of borrowing recklessly and not attending to his parochial duties. Eventually he decided to resolve his difficulty by renting Kilbride Cottage and going to live:

> ... in the old hotel in Blesinton, provided Lord Downshire will properly repair it. They will let their own pretty cottage with or without more ground and make by this about one hundred pounds a year, while they will save near another by buying all they want in the market instead of cultivating their forty acres at an outlay of two horses and four men. He will give up the Kilbride parish to a curate, or altogether if it can be disserved, and sell his property the moment land rises, so relieve himself of a load which is breaking his heart. And after the move is made he will be so much happier, doing his duty, knowing his income, and living amongst us all instead of only with his bees and roses.

Shortly after this, Elizabeth returned to the financial situation of the Moores and the Milltowns:

> ... When we think of some of our friends – the Ogle Moores – I feel that we are mercifully dealt with. The Steward and gardener are dismissed

> from Russborough – nearly all the labourers – and two maids – they must live on six hundred pounds a year and the farm. The Moores have two hundred and forty pounds for their income, all else being swallowed up by the interest of his personal debts. The property will not pay its own liabilities so it can give him nothing – his living he has encumbered most improperly by ensuring his life for a sum borrowed to relieve pressing difficulties – he has bonded debts besides, for he is acting like a madman. With this two hundred and forty pounds and eleven children they are keeping seven women servants and four outside men, and permit themselves every luxury and indulge in lives of utter indolence, neglect every duty, and say in tears 'what can we do'. Mrs Moore knows of every debt except the one to the Doctor yet she makes no exertions, gives up no indulgence, and he pets her up like a spoiled child. One feels ashamed of both of them, only we must recollect how very badly they were both brought up. What vicious sentiments they have always heard, what questionable habits they have always seen, and in Ogle's case I really believe his brain is not in order. My children laugh at me for calling every one mad who acts madly that is ill, but is it not madness to do wrong knowing right. In this case the family weakness clings to poor Ogle ... and the pride they are all puffed up with. People of their condition! With just four ancestors they can name on the father's side and zero on that score on the Mother's – like Lady Milltown and her peerage, bought in Mr Pitt's time, by a brewer!

Elizabeth later appeared to apportion most of the blame for the Rev. Moore's situation on his wife, saying she ought to have seen that:

> ... her husband was out of health, out of spirits, she ought to have asked herself whether their income warranted their expenditure, she ought to have attended more actively to her family, she ought never to have yielded to her unseemly habits of self-indulgence. Her children were frequently in rags, she had no lists of their clothing, no catalogue of furniture, no house book of expenses. She never bought an article, she never saw a bill. When shirts or shifts or bonnets or tea, or rice or beer was wanting, Ogle was told and Ogle ordered. Was it difficult to see the end.

Still on the subject of other people's difficulties, Elizabeth made a single reference to a Mr Gillhooly for whom a bankrupt sale had been conducted. Everything went cheap because of the depressed state of the economy and the general shortage of money:

> At the conclusion, the poor drunken body brought out the drunken wife and insisted with the auctioneer on her being canted [auctioned]: there was no bid. Irish fun even in ruin. What a curious people.

To the modern reader this scene may seem reminiscent of Thomas Hardy's *The Mayor of Casterbridge.* Instances of wives actually being auctioned have been recorded in 18th and 19th century England and the historian, E. P. Thompson, accepts as authentic 12 cases between 1800 and 1840 and 55 between 1840 and 1880. The practice seems to have functioned as an early form of popular divorce.[1]

The Smiths were continuing to have problems trying to sell-off surplus stock. In September, all the animals which they had sent to the fair at Rathsallagh came back without an offer being made for a single beast. Not only did this mean a loss of income but it also meant that the estate continued to incur the extra expense of continuing to feed the unsold stock. Writing about a filly which her husband was also unable to sell, she commented: 'when a horse is not wanted, it is a pity to be at the expense of feeding him'.

> Bankruptcy is facing us all; still, sagacious people say that after a year or two more of struggle, the prudent among us will more than receive former comfort. In the meantime, on marches ruin rapidly – in the South and West it has left little behind it, and here it comes upon us in this garden of Ireland. The system of carrying off the crops during the night in order to avoid the payment of rent has become quite general in the South and is even approaching us. Mr Reid is the first victim – he is deservedly unpopular; yet it is a horrid dishonest revenge.

Elizabeth continued to be grateful that she and Hal had been able to cope with the difficult times with a fair degree of success:

> We may be thankful we are so well off – grateful for our small independent income and satisfied with our own conduct in having so well retrieved the little landed property that it will provide for its own liabilities and perhaps begin, after another year, to give us something over as formerly, though only by degrees ...

Hopes that the year 1849 might see the end of the potato blight were dashed when, in August, the journal recorded that 'the blight has appeared on the potatoes, partially', adding that 'the trampers [itinerants] are stealing them night after night, seldom now calling for bread'. At the same time

1. See E.P. Thompson, *Customs in Common,* (London), pp. 404–62

she also recorded the sinister news of an outbreak of cholera locally. There had been plenty of sickness, much of it resulting from undernourishment. Her doctor had already told her about:

> ... bad accounts of fever and other exterminating diseases here. He had come upon a wretched group, a woman and children cowering over a smouldering fire in a plantation at the back of Russborough where they had passed the night – all ill – he had got a cart from Lord Milltown and sent them off to Naas. But sickness is so prevailing he has come round to the necessity of fitting up one Dispensary [in Blessington] as a fever hospital. If the gentlemen will subscribe for a nurse and provisions and fuel, we ladies will manage with the bedding and linen. Colonel Smith offers ten pounds, Mr West, ditto. Richard Hornidge and others don't see the necessity of any such measure.

In spite of the lack of universal support, the project to build Blessington hospital on the road to Naas actually went ahead. Now a private house, it was constructed by the same mason who built the market house in Blessington. Soon there were:

> nineteen patients glad to be received there, not as in former times, preferring to die at home and infect their whole family. The expense will come out of the whole county at large and what an amount of good results. First, the patients are surrounded with comforts, and get hourly visits from the doctors; next, infection is prevented from spreading, then fuel must be brought, washerwomen hired, nurse tenders paid ... They are all so satisfied with the results hitherto that they are thinking of branch wings for wounds, etc., a general hospital in fact.

* * *

The Smiths continued to live a quiet and relatively modest life-style and Elizabeth's circle of friends remained quite small. However, during July and August of 1849, there was a flurry of society events and visits which centred around both the royal visit of Queen Victoria to Dublin and the impending annual visit to his Blessington estate of the Marquis of Downshire, who resided for most of the year at Hillsborough, Co. Down. Long before Queen Victoria's first visit to Ireland, Elizabeth had made some very sardonic remarks about the royal personage. At the beginning of her Irish journal, she had commented on the young queen's speech at the opening of parliament, describing it as 'a sad silly speech – things of importance hardly touched on – about the weakest ever uttered of all those unmeaningful productions'. She recollected, as a little girl, having seen King George [the fourth] and Queen Charlotte, a memory that made her remark upon 'how much per cent has the value of royalty fallen since those times'. When Elizabeth read that Victoria and her family had gone to reside in Brighton, she posed the question: 'What on earth is the use of her to the nation?' She then elaborated:

> It is really a very expensive head ... of no use towards its government and for other purposes might really be curtailed of much of its importance, for the world is gradually rising above Court dangling and will not very long endure the extreme etiquette required there. When we are fit for further equality this magnificent remnant of barbarism will be laid aside like other worn out traditions.

In 1842, when a masked ball was organised for the queen, Elizabeth described it as 'a most ridiculous piece of mummery ... turning her Court into a Playhouse ... putting a mimick crown too on poor [Prince] Albert's head, who must often enough fret at his position so near it.' Earlier, a family friend had told of his visit to Queen Victoria at Windsor where he had dined with her and played whist .... 'She told him to see her children and [he] hid himself behind the nursery door to enjoy their surprise; he says they are not pretty children, but healthy, very plainly dressed'.

In 1847, Elizabeth had read that Victoria was about to 'yacht around her islands – can't sit still, poor restless young creature'. Two years later, Lady Downshire told Elizabeth's husband that the queen 'is still most violently in love with her husband, he is quite indifferent about her; a cold, quiet, not a clever man – a nobody. Her temper is very violent. She is not the least bit pretty now, nor by any means agreeable, never for one moment disqueening herself. She never descends from her high estate, nor suffers anyone else to forget it..

Anyway, this was the royal personage who was due to make her first visit to Ireland in August 1849. The Smiths, like almost everyone else, had been cutting out unnecessary expense in running both the estate and the household, so Elizabeth was very conscious of the expense likely to be involved in such a visit.

> Surely the Queen has chosen a most unhappy season for her first visit. It may put the nation into good humour perhaps, but it will fearfully encrease debts and difficulties. A little present worry for future cares. However, once in a way we must 'make an effort'. Make up our minds to it and go through it gallantly.

Many middle-class people and traders and even the wealthy continued to be seriously affected by the famine – not so much, in their case, because of a shortage of food on their tables but because there was a general shortage of money. Despite this, many of the better-off contrived to make the most of any social occasions and, of course, the anticipated royal visit. Elizabeth's description of some of the royal events during the summer of 1849 contrast vividly with the scenes she was witnessing in the cottages and hovels around her home.

Coincidentally, Lord Downshire's 1849 visit to Blessington, which had been timed to celebrate his birthday on 6 August, clashed with the royal visit to Dublin. When he arranged a Ball and supper for his friends and for all his tenantry, down-to-earth Elizabeth's comment was: 'It will do a deal of good to our rapidly declining county this six weeks of Downshire expenditure among us'.

Despite her earlier reservations, Elizabeth was just beginning to look forward to Queen Victoria's visit when her husband decided that, because of their financial situation, the family would not be joining in the celebrations. Elizabeth was, initially, very annoyed but on reflection reluctantly accepted Hal's decision:

> We are not to grace the royal festivities. The Colonel was undecided for some time, but on calculating the cost, he thinks it would be not only inconvenient but wrong in these times to incur such expense. I don't agree with him, I think our duty to our daughters requires this effort from us, and that we keep them beneath their proper position by not presenting them among the society they ought to belong to, for it is not only the court they lose but every entertainment made for her majesty, at none of which they can appear. Perhaps he is right, at any rate he is the master, so there is no more about it. I may be too vain or too ambitious, former recollections interfering with the poor Officer's wife; while he may err on the other side, having never mixed with the world in his early youth and going out to India before he was capable of understanding the fitness of form at home. He is also extremely shy, I am not pushing, both too proud and too indolent, but I know my own place and I should like if possible to keep my girls in it. But it is not to be. They had set their young hearts on it, having now a large dancing acquaintance among really nice people and they had been settling their dresses with the Lady Leesons, who are full of it too. It is a good trial – and so Adieu.

As some kind of compensation for this disappointment, Elizabeth had some more lively news to report about the impending visit of the

Downshires:

> Such commotion this day in the little town of Blesinton. Instead of arriving next week as the Marquis of Downshire had pre-arranged, a letter came this morning to say he and wife and children and servants and governess and secretary and all appurtenances would be here on Wednesday. The whole county is astir, for the tenantry, three hundred in number, are to meet the carriages on the boundary of the property, on horse and foot, and escort the young heir into the village, which is to be illuminated from one end to the other in the evening. In truth this good landlord is much beloved and well worthy of every mark of respect from his people and indeed from his neighbours, for no man could be more really good-natured.

She continued to write about the impending royal visit and of her two daughters' disappointment at Hal's decision that the family would forego the celebrations in Dublin. Elizabeth's girls 'walked til ten o'clock in the Avenue, informing the young plantations of their griefs'. An early example, perhaps, of talking to the trees? Still ruminating about her husband's decision and her daughter's disappointment she wrote:

> The Colonel is seldom wrong when he takes the trouble to think. It may be best for our girls to remain in an humble station, they have not fortunes to warrant their abiding among the great; so my dream of vanity and ambition without leaving any particular impression of spirits behind. The girls themselves have really had a pouting fit about it, for the first time in their lives as far as I have observed ... a certain grandeur of manner, paucity of conversation and an air of resignation to ill usage which, very amusingly, was assumed to punish contumacious parents. The Doctor made matters worse, for he is so absurd about the children that he thinks them fit to sit upon the throne beside Queen Victoria herself with all their nobles of the land at their feet.

There was some compensation for Elizabeth and her daughters when they received an invitation to the Downshires' Ball, and Elizabeth decided to take a look at the preparations:

> Went into Blesinton to see all the cooking going on in the old hotel, four bullocks, twenty sheep, lambs, hams and five cwt of plum pudding all preparing there under the charge of an old messman, quite up to the thing and very much delighted with the bustle and his guinea a day.

A few days later, Elizabeth described in some detail what had happened at the event:

> All very tired after the Ball which went off pretty well, one thousand five hundred tenantry and peasantry dined in the old hotel, the five rooms upstairs each contained two tables laid for forty or forty four, the elite of the company, three rooms on the ground floor similarly arranged were for the second rank, and all the mountaineers were at fourteen tables in the vaults. The large room, now undivided, was prepared for dancing, but it being insufficient each room turned into a ballroom after the supper, pipers and fluters being plenty. The schoolhouse was used as a ballroom by the labourers, and in almost every publick house there was dancing, besides an immense crowd about the bonfire in the market place, which mob, owing to the rain, got very unmannerly and tried to force their way into the hotel. Numbers succeeded, making a rush every time the door opened, though two gentlemen and two yeomen were stationed in the passage to prevent them.
>
> The rain was extremely unfortunate as it prevented all the fun we Selects had promised ourselves in visiting the different places of amusement. The gentlemen indeed braved the weather, leaving the few ladies collected in the market house to enjoy the excellent musick of Kavanagh's Band without any chance of dancing to it, for they were wanted to keep order in the hotel, carve for the awkward, serve the drink and so on, and they served too much drink as, long before midnight there was hardly a sober man and long before daybreak there were hundreds drunken. It was wonderful that no accident happened among them; the gentlemen and a few others kept order. Our party was hurt by the Queen, so many had gone in to see her enter Dublin. She was enthusiastically received, showed herself most gracefully and abundantly and was in right good humour. She has grown very fat, was much sun-burned, and too plainly dressed to please the Irish. As she did not come in state there was no procession to signify. The illuminations must have been quite spoiled by the rain. To-day she visits all that is worth seeing in the city.

Elizabeth then reverted to her description of how the Downshire's Ball had been opened 'by a country dance' and her daughters persuaded their parents to cross the street from the Market House to the hotel to see the goings-on for themselves; Elizabeth was carried across by John Hornidge and Mr Wolfe to Mrs Owen's house, where she 'went at once to bed'. On the following Sunday, after attending church service in Blessington, Elizabeth heard further accounts of the royal visit to Dublin, and how it had gone off 'brilliantly':

> The Drawing-room [of the Vice-regal Lodge] frightfully crowded, but owing to the presentations at the Ball the night before, the Queen made quicker work than she was able to do at the *Levee*. There were three dinners at the Park, followed by an evening party, a Ball and a concert, then the Review and Drawing-room, after leaving which her Majesty embarked for the north. The Leesons were at the Ball. The Queen was in high good humour during her visit, everything went off so well, no mistakes, no annoyances, and brilliant weather. Her Prince is a sad stick, not even appearing to be interested at the Agricultural Show, where he merely walked about with a very indifferent air and left as soon as might be. He is a young man very much to be pitied to my mind.

A few days after this, Elizabeth got a detailed, first-hand report Lady Milltown when she visited Russborough the following week:

> Lord Milltown had been given the entree at the Levee, privately, on account of his infirmity, they were all asked to the private ball, and Lady Milltown was one of the two Countesses among the twenty selected guests who dined at the Queen's table. Lady Milltown thinks nobody handsome and no woman well dressed, but her girls told mine it was one blaze of beauty and perfect toilettes and they heard the English suite were amazed at the air of all, person, costume and manner alike distinguished. Lord Downshire did the honours of the north and found her Majesty most gracious.

During the month of August, the Smiths paid a visit to Powerscourt. Presumably they travelled by Manor Kilbride to the Sally Gap, across the Liffey Head (at an altitude of over 1,700 feet) and down through Glencree. Elizabeth wrote the following account in her diary:

> Such a journey, fifty two English miles. The lawn was extensive, the wooding beautiful, the views all the way up so pretty; then we passed the neat church, then a sort of dressed farmyard, and then came out upon the house, the Custom House on the Quay at Dublin transplanted to the country. I don't myself like this style of architecture, too formal, nor can I endure these palaces with their stiff gravel terraces amid the natural beauties of trees, fields, hills and ocean; but the place as a place is fine, the house as a work of art, handsome, and the interiour of it a

> shew and a shew only, for no one with simple happy tastes could endure to live in rooms so gorgeous.
>
> Powerscourt is very beautiful and we saw it to great advantage, house and grounds having been put in order for the Queen. She had intended to visit it with a view to selecting it for her residence on her future visits, but time failed her. I am certainly not intended by nature to live among the great for I could not exist at Powerscourt. I could not settle myself with my book or my work in any of those splendid rooms, not can I fancy anyone enjoying existence in these golden fetters. No opening window leads to flowers, a long gravel walk on a stone terrace must be traversed before a shrub or plant is reached. Satin dresses, satin shoes, scents and ceremonies belong to those courtly rooms, the toys of the child and the occupations of a rational being would be equally out of place there. The beauty of the scenery is spoiled by the many villas which the near neighbourhood of Dublin has crowded the ground with.

Just a few days after this, Elizabeth reluctantly accepted an invitation from Lady Milltown to join her whole family for a day-trip to Glendalough and back – a journey of some 40 miles – twice traversing the Wicklow Gap. Considering the kind of roads in those days, and that carriages had no effective lights, it seems surprising that they did not set out on the journey home until after mid-night:

> ... off to the Seven Churches, all but the Colonel who did not dare to venture. It was a lovely day and a very pleasant party quite unlike what we expected. There was a good and a merry dinner, a lounging walk, a tea, a boating and a charming moonlight drive home. Lord Downshire was my Beau during the ramblings, and for most of the hilly road home and very pleasant he is, altogether it was a highly agreeable day. Lady Milltown behaved wonderfully well and did her best to make her party go off well. At one time she was disposed to be a little hoity toity but, nobody minding her, she sobered down, her girls manage her admirably and as for the conduct of Edward to his father [the Earl of Milltown], it is so unobtrusively devoted as to be beautiful; they are the best children in the world.

* * *

Although they had also been to several other functions, this high society living was somewhat uncharacteristic of the normally relatively quiet life at Baltiboys House. A friend (the Doctor) told the Smiths of his recent

The old Burgage Bridge, demolished prior to the flooding of the valley in 1939, when the date-stone (inscribed 1767) was removed to Manor Kilbride.

St Mark's Cross at Burgage was also removed in 1939, and re-sited nearer to Blessington. It may originally have been dedicated to Malchus, twelfth century archbishop of Glendalough. (Séamas Ó Maitiú)

visit to the Marquis of Downshire at his stately home in County Down:

> Very different was Hillsborough! The Downshires live in regal state. Servants innumerable, silent as the grave, let you want for nothing, plate to no end. The cook shining, eating all day, dinners to twenty, hot luncheons, breakfasts beyond perfection, immense house, corridors and staircases and passages with bedrooms so luxuriously furnished, and all full. Besides which company staying, there were crowds arrived to the private plays and the ball and the concert; many pleasant people and some beautiful girls. My Lord a very kind host. My Lady too careless to do the honours well generally. Both made plenty of the Doctor, who certainly enjoyed his visit much. Yet the philosopher carries the day; he says he would not lead such a life for twice the fortune, so unsatisfactory, so fatiguing, such a parade of wealth added to ceremony to get vain mortals one day nearer to the grave.
>
> I have another way of thinking of all this, the good it does, the tradesmen employed – the servants required; the provisions consumed. The use in the neighbourhood, enlivening society, polishing it, improving it in many ways and bringing people together. I have no wish to act the princely host, but I should like very well to belong to the courtly circle when good feeling guided the proceedings of the centre of it. We miss that sort of *palace* in this country, there is no one to reign over us, so we get cross and stupid and *savage* and some of us impertinent.

For the Smiths there were occasional visits to Dublin. The recently-built railway line between the capital and Cork conveniently passed through Sallins, about a dozen miles away, making access to the capital more agreeable.

> Yesterday, being a beautiful morning, and there being several little things to do in Dublin, Papa, Mama, and Jack got up at half after five, breakfasted, the girls getting up to see us off, drove to Sallins, and there took seats in a railroad carriage. Beautiful line of rail, neat stations, handsome carriages, fine rich country all the way to Dublin by Hazelhatch, Celbridge, Lucan, plenty of gentlemen's seats.[1] A wonderful promise for harvest which is already begun, several fields were full of reapers. We got in an hour, nearly, to the terminus, an immense building, though not so extensive as the Company's factory [the Inchicore Railway Engineering Works], a mile from the end, round which they have quite

1. The Great Southern aand Western Railway Company opened its Dublin to Cork line as far as Carlow in 1846

> a village of neat houses for all the various people they employ, some of whom are quite gentlemen. The clerk, who took our tickets, had the manners and the hands of high breeding.

Two years earlier, on another visit to Dublin, Elizabeth had remarked on the effects of the famine upon the metropolis, a reminder of the widespread consequences of the disaster. This was her description of the scene as she and her husband reached the suburbs:

> ... only melancholy evidences of the distress were to be met with – every second house to be let – of those retreats where the Dublin tradesmen lived with their families, neat small places with carsheds beside them, little gardens in front and green fields behind. I began to count the number of shops shut up as we advanced and got to twenty six by the time we reached the entrance of the busy part of the City. The shops are deserted. One or two we had to enter, we were alone in, few shopmen either, there being nothing for them to do and they offered us their goods for anything we chose to give them, like cheap bread to those who cannot earn its value. This was useless to me, I had to lay out the least possible sum required by our necessities, so I had to look on what was tempting with the same eyes as would one dying of hunger on a heap of diamonds.

The part played by the over-dependence of so many upon the potato was often the subject of Elizabeth's attention, and she summed up the situation which faced the country in October, 1849 thus:

> A cheap market in a commercial country appears to me to encourage improvidence and imprudence. In the potato days of Ireland, the poor rushed into the most reckless marriages, economised nothing, thought of nothing, prepared for nothing, improved in nothing. The entire failure of their cheap food has checked marriage and all the train of its ills following this unwise piece of profligacy, which is the true epithet of a pauper wedlock.

In November, following a prolonged period of very bad weather, the journal recorded:

> A fine day at last to cheer us, a bright sun. It really was too depressing to be groping about under that dark sky while the gloom of increasing poverty was paralysing all mental energy. Wretched land, what suffering the most meritorious of its inhabitants are undergoing, all more or less

> stricken and no prudence on the part of the wiser able to secure them against the pressure of the evils resulting from the want of principle of the improvident. All share alike in the general bankruptcy. I often pray that my senses may be preserved to me, and that my health of mind and body may stand this struggle, and aid me to preserve an invalid husband and our dear children from much of the real poverty round them – they miss their luxuries – necessaries they still have and will have, our British money [the Colonel's pension] will ever secure us a sufficient supply of them – but the want of enough to help to relieve others is a painful part of these unhappy times. To keep our own people from starving absorbs all there is to spare.

Elizabeth's journal repeatedly makes it clear that she thought good landlords were very much in the minority, but it should be said that almost all landlords, good, bad and indifferent at this time, were themselves severely affected by the famine. It is probably also true to say that the majority of landlords lacked the skills needed to properly manage their estates, thus rendering them all the more vulnerable to the effects of the famine as matters got worse. More progressive landlords, like Colonel Smith, had already been in the process of attempting to consolidate their estates by arresting the seemingly endless process of division and sub-division of land. Colonel Smith also saw the advantages of undertaking drainage works and introuducing new crops (he was the first to grow turnips in the area). However, raising productivity and economising wherever possible was simply not enough at a time of rapidly rising prices, when arrears and non-payment of rents drastically reduced so many landlords' incomes. The position of the landlords was further aggravated when the government decided to force them to bear the main burden of famine relief, a move which presented them with an added incentive to ride their estates of unwanted or 'troublesome' tenants.

Writing in *The Irish Times* about Coole Park, the home of Lady Gregory, Nuala O'Faolain, expressed the view that 'landlord history is a distinct and very interesting layer of our history', a layer which, it might be added, has been largely neglected. Given the awfulness and the scale of the famine, it is hardly surprising that, even one hundred and fifty years later, it continues to be controversial to make any kind of case on behalf of the landlords, although it is obvious that almost everyone else in a position to do so made the most of every available opportunity to either enrich or protect themselves. As Elizabeth Smith noted in her journal, traders and shopkeepers raised the prices of scarce food to the point where the starving poor could not afford to buy, and middlemen were no less ruthless with their own tenants than the landlords from whom they in turn rented their land. Surely it is valid to at least speculate whether the motivations of the landlords in getting rid of as many tenants as possible greatly differed from the motivations of today's businessmen who dismiss what they perceive to be their surplus staff in their quest for greater economy or survival.

While it is almost impossible to assess accurately the numbers of tenants evicted during the famine years, one thing that is certain is that the numbers continued to increase steadily from 1845 to 1850 Also, the wholesale evictions in certain areas, such as parts of Ulster and Counties Tipperary and Leitrim, may well have contributed to the perception that the numbers were even worse than they actually were. One source states that in the worst year the total represented only 2.5 per cent of all agricultural holdings.

The level of suffering varied considerably from county to county and Wicklow, along with Dublin and much of Ulster, emerged as one of the more fortunate areas. But as Elizabeth Smith's journal makes clear, even within this relatively well-off county, conditions could be markedly different locally; she noted that areas like Baltinglass, Hollywood and Dunlavin presented scenes of abject misery while Blessington and Baltiboys escaped relatively lightly. But even this latter generalisation is misleading as individual tenants on her own estate were among those who suffered greatly.

It may seem surprising then that towards the end of 1849, during 'the same most abominable weather – rain for ever, so dark one can hardly see', Elizabeth recorded that the Smiths had:

> ... the pleasantest rent day, yesterday, that we have had since the famine year. Not only did the tenants pay well but they looked happy – no complaints, no demands, no shuffling – a half year's rent and a pleased air in giving it, was offered by all but three who will pay up the difference by Christmas. Some even paid a portion of their arrears. They say it is the draining which has brought them through; money in hand for labour they had no call for, and time given them, and care taken of them, and kindness shown them. We deserve their attachment and I really do think we have it.

As is already evident, Elizabeth's moods could quickly change from optimism to despondency Not long after the above came this entry:

> Such harassing times. Between our own distresses and our friends', it is really difficult to keep up our spirits. I have had no time for the journal, some quiet half hour I must run over matters, they will tell a tale for other years.

1850

"The starving children are looking better already"

The New Year soon saw hard frost lying over the recently fallen snow. The skies were dark and gloomy, Colonel Smith had bronchitis and his wife had both influenza and a 'slight attack of liver'. However, as she commented, the weather was seasonable and 'healthy and very good for the ground' Later, after a visit to Edinburgh to see her mother and sister, she returned home to 'the Wicklow Hills' where she found all the familiar scenes of famine distress around her.

> We have kept the people in our immediate neighbourhood alive these two years and now they must die, or beg, or steal, any thing rather than the Poor House which, however, must be full for we give no outdoor relief in this Union and our rates, though lighter on us than they were last year, are still heavy. Sheep are beginning to disappear. We have lost one which, considering all we have done to lessen the distress, is a bad sign. Sam Darker lost five sheep, Mr West two, one of them a prize for which he gave a high price. We must be careful in our expenditure as probably the few small tenants we have may be induced to emigrate if assisted, Lachlin and Mary Ryan are gone to New Orleans with a large party of friends, Mary under the charge of Kiogh the tailor's son and wife. We paid all her expenses and most of her brother's; he had a little money, the Doctor gave him a suit of old clothes, the Colonel did the remainder; Annie superintended the whole affair and did it all properly. Even in a business point of view this is a £10 profitably laid out.

Ten days later, she wrote that the Magistrates had sent some local people to jail for sheep stealing:

> ... the two McKayes for our sheep, and a man of the name of Pearson who stole three or four, and three wretched girls who took two from Dizest; plundering is going on all round us, fifteen hundred in the

Poor House, yet we are infested with beggars. More of Lord Milltown's plate gone to be sold, and peers and gentles going down down down, never to rise again. ... God help the people, the roads are beset with tattered skeletons, they give one a shudder to look at, for how can we feed or clothe so many.

The Smiths continued to demonstrate concern for their own tenants; Elizabeth, with her husband and younger daughter, visited some of them in February, including:

... three old women; poor creatures they think themselves comfortable, so they are by comparison, but all is very wretched. Made up a bundle for one of them that good Miss Macdonald carried home. She is in the schoolhouse living and will soon have her bare room neat, she is both managing and tidy. I declare the starving children look better already.

The situation of one of the 'difficult' tenant families came nearer to resolution at the end of February when the Grays finally decided to give up possession of their holding. The old man:

... asked nothing; threw himself on the Colonel's liberality and said he had a few bits of good furniture to sell which would help him. The manure he considers due to the ground instead of the half-years' rent; so the Colonel will give him five pounds and one pound to that wretched Kitty if they will take her with them.

Elizabeth's diary entries now began to become more irregular – sometimes for want of 'remarkable events' but more often because she was busier than ever writing articles for publication in order to supplement the family's income. As she put it on one such occasion: 'My private talk with the poor dear neglected journal must wait a wee'. Another reason was the engagement, in March, of her daughter Annie, soon to be followed by the preparations for the wedding at the end of the year. There was also a problem caused by the decision to allow the farm steward to 'take' land. The details are obscure – but it annoyed some of the tenants and Elizabeth felt the transaction was a mistake. The row apparently broke out over the decision to allow the steward, Tom Darker, to farm part of the land formerly farmed by the Smiths themselves. Elizabeth wrote that the decision had:

... raised a most unpleasant feeling among the people, one that will be difficult to allay; the transaction was a mistake, but we must now let

> them beard us .... Not a man in Baltiboys is the worse for Tom Darker cultivating these patches on his own account instead of on the Colonel's. What business is it of theirs? There is another sore subject with them which I can better understand their ill humour on – the drainage loan; though the redeemed loan puts many a pound into their pockets they can't abide paying a few extra shillings for this. I wish they were all in America, I know.

In May, Elizabeth described the pathetic scenes of emigrants travelling the road to Dublin on the first leg of their long journey to try to start a new life abroad:

> ... the better sort emigrating with money, leaving the Paupers of all classes at home to starve together. It is melancholy really to walk along the roads the day before the steamer sails for America; such crowds followed the poor wretched carts with the rickety luggage in it, all the women in tears, all the men surly, and yet they leave want behind and have hope before them.

A few months earlier, Elizabeth had read an account of a tragedy which struck an emigrant ship:

> A Sligo steamer bound for Liverpool put into Derry from stress of weather and landed seventy-two corpses. The crew had shut down the hatches on the miserable steerage passengers, all emigrants bound for America, and suffocated half of them. Captain, etc. are in jail.

* * *

The rents became due again on 1 June and the journal shows that the tenants paid 'really well'

> We received about half [of] the half year's rents, but more will come in the course of a month or so; the principle defaulter is Rutherford who has not brought one penny. No tenant save him owes a years rent. Some few we are owed a half year; others are short only by a few pounds of paying up the full term. We ought to be quite satisfied.

In July, Elizabeth described a walk around part of the estate when she went:

> on the hill in the morning looking after the new cottages [and then]

walked with Tom Darker all over the upper part of Judy Ryan's old farm which he is bringing into fine order and laid out a plan for the Commons' 'ill-used acres'.

Elizabeth returned to the topic of the new cottages or 'cabins' a few weeks later:

> Not at all lime enough in the floors and old shabby windows that won't open, with only four panes in them. We must have hinges put on to them at any rate; and the demand for a little scrap of a flower garden, shall be complied with – gladly. This is owing to Lady Downshire's move; the neat gardens already blooming before so many of her cottages, and perhaps her intended flower show and premiums have spirited up her neighbours; the country is improving.

When their neighbouring friends, Mr and Mrs George West, called to tell of their plans to visit the Giant's Causeway in County Antrim, the cattle show in Cork and how they then spent a month in Roscommon, Elizabeth was far from impressed:

> How people scrape up money for such vagaries these times is a matter of wonder to me, and how the parents of four nice children can leave them to servants and go wandering about for no reason but pleasure is still a greater amazement to those who are brought up to do their duty and find their happiness at home.

The harvest prospects in mid-July appeared good: 'Such corn and hay and potatoes as we have not seen for many a day and difficult to get people for field labour. Eight turnip weeders after searching the country and we have to take them off to make the hay. Two mowers only; so here is the rain before the heavy crop is safe'. On the first day of August, however, Elizabeth recorded that the potato disease had partially begun once again. 'A whole field touched here and there but generally only in patches as if the blight had swept across particular portions, and hitherto only the leaves and stalks are affected, it has not yet descended to the tubers'. A week later she wrote that 'the potatoes are failing again, the sight and smell of the disease is all around us'.

With little of interest going on in the neighbourhood, Elizabeth's now irregular journal entries seemed to be primarily concerned with the doings of her neighbours and the Blessington gossip. How the Marquis of Downshire had arrived unexpectedly from the north, is a typical instance:

> [He had] found nothing to eat – no servants arrived – Mrs Owen in her

room – Mr Owen away – the Doctor out. So he got Charlie to do him some rashers and eggs on which he dined; next day the Marchioness, straight from Germany and, after a kind greeting, my Lord went back to London to fetch over the children, and in the morning my Lady went up to Dublin to shop. Really these flighty ways sound queer to quiet people.

Following a visit to Russborough after Lady Milltown's father, Sir Joshua Meredith, had died Elizabeth wrote:

> Poor Lady Milltown, what a weak woman she is in some points. She is so anxious to make herself out years too young, therefore very angry with the newspapers for mentioning her father's age; he was indeed very old, and she is old enough as all the world well knows ...

As ever, if Elizabeth observed the faults of others she was not blind to those of her own. After recalling 'the merry days' when she was young, her 'highland days filled with a regular bustle of fun', she somewhat moodily compared all that with the situation of her own daughters:

> My poor girls have no fun; their life is really dull; nothing can exceed the utter stupidity of this neighbourhood, besides the Colonel and I are intensely stupid ourselves; he never cared for anything but hunting, rather indeed avoided society and I was too well pleased to be quiet, to attempt to counteract his indolent shyness; then our income is small and two thirds being spent outside the house very little was left for within, so Annie had married early.

After her husband had been unwell, Elizabeth thought a trip to Jersey would be good for him so he went in September with their son Jack. Elizabeth travelled to Dublin to see them off on a steamer going to Southampton which was also taking Irish emigrants on the first leg of their journey to Australia:

> There were few Cabin passengers but a shipload of Australian emigrants, decent looking people well supplied with luggage whose Adieux to the crowd which accompanied them to the Quay was a miserable scene to look at. Tears, sobs, screams even, with hystericks and fainting. To their class, the parting is final and though utter desolation is left, and hope shines bright before, the moment of separation from kindred and country must be painful to agony. I felt lonely enough as the vessel moved away, the poor Colonel leaning forward on the rail as

> the easiest posture for his asthma, and little Jack, in the grey shooting coat too short in the sleeves for his growth, standing by the helm looking wistfully after me. He has been too much with me, depended too much on me, he must now be prepared for his solitary battle with life, he will fight it gallantly or I am much mistaken. It was amusing to see the sort of charge he took of his father, his activity in looking after the portmanteaus, the head was higher by an inch.

Ironically, the Colonel returned from Jersey 'really looking well' but Jack came home 'like a corpse – he frightened me'.

Emigration caused Elizabeth to consider closing the boys' section of Baltiboys school; 'there are very few boys left on our side of the country; there will be few men soon for they are pouring in shoals to America.' A Mr McDarby had taken over the teaching of the boys remaining on the roll in 1849 and she describes him as:

> ... an intelligent young man, a native of Athy, educated in a National school from the beginning and trained in the Teacher's class in Marlborough Street [teacher training college in Dublin], he was never a probationer, nor a third class teacher, but at once started second class and got two removes in one year. He taught two years in a school of Lord Stanley's at Doon and brings a high character with him from the agent on that estate. He has been the two last years at Stratford under a *priest*, which, though a Roman Catholic, don't suit him.

Elizabeth Smith felt a little peeved when she discovered that McDarby had a young lady in his life, also a teacher, but he had not told her of this when he applied for the job. She would not have minded a married couple but, as he had described himself as a bachelor, she had employed another young lady to teach in Baltiboys.

McDarby highly amused Elizabeth while he was in Baltiboys. While he acknowledged his attachment to the young lady teacher of his acquaintance, he stated that he would marry anyone Elizabeth would chose for him whose temper was suitable and could bring 'her fair share of income with her'. When Elizabeth declined to act as matchmaker he struck up an acquaintance with the laundry-maid of the Rev. Ogle Moore, Rector of Blessington, a widow much older than himself with a child. They each declared themselves to be a good catch for the other, he having a good job, a house and land from Col. Smith and an 'estate in the Queen's County', she having money saved and furniture ready. When these claims turned out to be 'vapourings', as Elizabeth described them, the relationship abruptly ended. Elizabeth called McDarby a 'flighty fool, very soft on the women' and, despite his being too much given to beating the schoolchildren, she regarded him as a good teacher. In 1850 when he was ill in hospital, Elizabeth considered closing his school.

Tulfarris, the home of one of the two Hornidge famiiles in the neighbourhood. Elizabeth once commented that Mr Hornidge 'employs very few servants'. (Séamas Ó Maitiú)

Humphrystown House, situated about five miles from Baltiboys, where James King lived. He married Elizabeth Smith's younger daughter Annie, in 1850. (Dermot James)

With only two brief references to the blight during 1850, it is difficult to judge the extent of the disease and its consequences locally from Elizabeth's journal. She had mentioned the murder in County Roscommon of Major Denis Mahon at the end of 1847, and she was well aware of the deep resentment shown by tenants to many landlords during these terrible years. Once again, when there was trouble elsewhere, she fervently hoped that it would not spread to Baltiboys. She had been very concerned about the possible spread of political unrest to County Wicklow around the time of the Smith O'Brien insurrection in 1848 but in the meantime the sheer desperation of large numbers of starving people, allied with the growing demand for land reform, meant that desperate people were taking the law into their own hands, maiming landlords' stock, stealing sheep and crops and sometimes committing murder. As Elizabeth expressed it in the autumn of 1850, 'burglary and murder are as every day occurrences about London as crop lifting and murder are here'.

Some weeks after this, one of their neighbours, Mrs West, gave the Smiths a 'really most frightful account' of the unsettled state of some parts of the country:

> Major Mahon's cousin, Ross Mahon, has received several threatening letters. Those gentlemen [landlords],who remain in Roscommon have kept a guard of police about them, armed themselves and their protestant servants, and worn shirts of chain armour.

* * *

Around the same time, the Smiths became dissatisfied with John Byrne, their blacksmith, whose workmanship with the carriage horses was, they felt sure, the cause of at least one of them going lame. They then engaged a second smith, a man named Perry, and at first all went well:

> But yesterday he [Perry] said he must give the job up, he had been so threatened, and such calumnies had been circulated through Baltiboys regarding his ignorance of his trade. The very same feeling that leads to murders in those parts of the country where the vindictive propensities of the people are not kept under by resident protestant gentry of high character. The Colonel is not a man to be frightened: he settled matters summarily enough; he announced he should employ what tradesmen he pleased and that if his servants attempted to annoy any such as he thought fit to send for, he could change the servants just as easily as he had done his smith; that he had not taken the farm horses from John Byrne as yet thinking him sufficiently skillful in those departments, but

> that if he heard another syllable falsely derogating from the abilities of Perry, from that moment he should dismiss Byrne altogether. Everyone has since exculpated himself from having taken any part in these malignities and I hope the mischief is over.
>
> The Baltiboys people are so interconnected, intermarried, that in offending one we offend all and up they all start as if no one had a right to act towards any of them but just as the whole junta please. I was once served much the same on changing a laundry maid and had to announce that sooner than take the old one back I would wash the clothes myself, before any peace was given to her successor.

In September, news came of an assault made against a process server (bailiff), Tom Lees, who had been:

> ... in the discharge of his duty, set upon by men, women and children at Humfreystown bridge [Humphrystown lies a few miles south of Baltiboys] and cruelly beaten, mercifully not wounded, although some of his assailants were armed with pitchforks and reaping hooks. Lady Downshire and Miss Owen were driving home from the moors in a jaunting car and came across this frightful assemblage, enough to frighten any woman and it did much excite her but she drove on for rescue, sent some men off [and] went on to Blesinton for the police ....
>
> These unhappy people are just becoming as ill conducted in this neighbourhood once so peaceable, as they have long been elsewhere. A gathering of three or four hundred is no longer uncommon to cut and carry off crops in the night, ill-use keepers, and in all ways defy decency. And neither the Government nor the magistrates take the slightest cognisance of these outrages. A spirit of discontent is brewing all round us and must end in something unpleasant if not checked. The girls and I have been paying visits among the tenantry and I don't at all like the tone of some. I would gladly improve the condition of all, but am more inclined to help the hopeful than the desponding and we must, if possible, get quit of the sulky.

This increasing sense of lawlessness led to the establishment a few years later of a police barracks in Baltiboys; an unlikely place for one, as it is not in any sense a centre of population but was, in all probability, obtained through the influence of the Smith family.

What was to become of Rutherford, the tenant farmer who lived a few miles west of Baltiboys and who consistently failed to pay his rent? Elizabeth mentioned him four times during September and October:

> The Baltiboys tenantry have not paid badly considering the times. Rutherford's conduct is scandalous. He owes a year and a half's rent now, and the half year we took in kind was not worth half the money it represented. We shall eject him in November, at the loss of the winter's rent for no one will come in upon a farm at that season here, though it is the proper time to enter on husbandry. Two hundred and thirty pounds odd is no joke to lose in these struggling days. The poor old man would gladly go to America to his sons whose roguery seems to be prospering with them and, as the Colonel will leave him what property he may still have, he could take near a hundred pounds out to the farm but the wretched woman, the cause of the downfall of this decent family, declares she will not move; she may indeed stay here but not at Elverstown.

Three days later, the journal recorded that Rutherford would not give further trouble:

> Besides being well-meaning himself, he has a sensible friend, an Attorney, who is giving him good advice. It will end, I hope, in his taking the Colonel's liberal offer by the accepting of which he may carry about a hundred pounds to America. The old woman of course, is against this as she has been against every thing else that was right. He has paid dearly for the false steps.

About three weeks after this, the Smiths got almost twenty five pounds from the sale of Rutherford's hay and a few days later, on a cold frosty morning, she wrote that:

> ... we have had to send poor Rutherford cold comfort on it, in the shape of an Attorney's letter. He will stick by his ruined farm keeping himself a beggar and seriously inconveniencing us, when he might carry a hundred pounds in his pocket to America, and end his days in comfort among his prospering children there.

So many people emigrated but so little was to be heard about most of them subsequently. Two years earlier, there had been a journal reference to a letter from Jim Doyle – 'one of those miserable people upon the hill.' He had emigrated to America in 1847 and had written home to say that, on arrival, his uncle there 'had met him on the quay and had two suits of clothes ready for him as people must be well dressed in that country'. Doyle was now working in a factory for twenty shillings a week which prompted Elizabeth to speculate on the outcome if 'the poverty stricken parents let this well-doing lad alone or let him really help them by sending, by and bye, for a brother or sister ....'

Elizabeth subsequently referred to letters from two other Baltiboys tenants who had also gone to America. One of these concerned Mary Ryan, who, with Lachlin, had earlier in the year gone 'with a large party of friends' to New Orleans. The Smiths had paid all Mary's expenses and most of her brothers' too and Elizabeth noted after they had gone that 'these orphans who have much plagued us will cost us no more, and they may act as pioneers for their numerous relations'.

In the letter, Mary Ryan had written that she and her brother 'were in service' and they had continued thus ever since their arrival. 'Lachlan has his board and a pound a week – Mary her board and lodging and a pound a month' The letter indicated that they were both happy and they were anxious for their friends to follow them. When Nancy Fox, a tenant whose two sons had also emigrated, received a letter from Cincinnati stating that both were doing well, Elizabeth remarked that 'the numbers gone are quite countless, and the countless numbers going are beyond all calculation, yet the wretchedness is dreadful ....'

* * *

This was to be one of the last references made by Elizabeth to the misery and wretchedness caused by the famine. She had repeatedly described the situation throughout the famine years and she must have found it difficult to avoid a monotonous repetition. But, in the closing weeks of 1850, there were indications that, however bad the situation, the worst was now over:

> I was hours making up bundles of patches and rags and old clothes for distributing among the poor who are certainly not so numerous as they used to be, though their wretchedness is extreme ...

And, on 25 December there was a very long entry, part of which went as follows:

> Christmas Day. It is years since the thought of a merry Christmas crossed a mind of late, almost sad at this so-called cheerful time. This year I feel the season's worth...
> All off to church this beautiful Christmas morning, the Colonel the gayest of the party. Ever since his visit to St. Fentons he has been in tip top spirits, quite like his own younger days, and he is so well, so alive, so awake, it really makes the heart glad to see him. On the 19th., Friday, at the school where we were entertaining all our little pupils

> with tea and bread and butter and the Piper, each dancing – thumping rather – and such slices of bread and butter, some of them equal in size to the heads of the devourers; the tea was made in a pot and two kettles and looked black enough. The neatness of the children was remarkable, all quite clean, hair very smooth, no tawdry finery but good, decent clothing; how very different from what we can remember of those poor ragged creatures.

* * *

For some time, the young James King had been paying attention to Annie, the Smith's younger daughter, and Elizabeth admitted, on the first occasion she had mentioned this, that she did not know what to make of him or 'whether to like him or no'.

> He is an only son and has evidently been spoiled. But I can't make up my mind about him. He seems too good to be discouraged if his attentions have any meaning; if they have not, he deserves banishment for he is making our dear sweet Annie very remarkable, singling her out on all occasions ... Were I once satisfied about his character, either for good or evil, I would know what to do.

Elizabeth's main concern was that Annie was, when this affair started in the summer of 1849, only seventeen years of age so she informed him that Annie would not be allowed to marry until they were both twenty. Six months later, Mr King (as Elizabeth continued to call him) was continuing to visit Annie and Elizabeth admitted in her journal that she found herself unable 'to prevail to have them discontinued' adding that while she liked him, 'I don't think him deserving of Annie'. However, as time went by, Annie's parents gradually relented: 'Our little Annie is very happy and the lover is very near heaven' she wrote sometime later and, even before the important matter of determining the suitor's financial prospects had been finalised, Elizabeth was referring to James King as 'our son-in-law'. She then confided to her journal: 'I do think that my dearly loved Annie will be safe in his hands and that they will be happy together' That she eventually came to terms with the situation is evident from the following entry:

> I should have liked to have kept Annie a few years longer unmarried ... but regrets are vain, the thing is done and I am relieved to find with some weaknesses, plenty of brains, a kind heart, a cheerful temper and the manners and the feelings of a gentleman.

There is insufficient space here, and it would not be appropriate to the general content of this volume, to detail Elizabeth's marvellous descriptions of the preparations for her daughter's marriage to James King. She chronicled the invitation list, the bride's 'wardrobe' (which included eighteen pairs of drawers), all the wedding presents (one of which was accompanied by an exclamation mark) and a full description of the wedding festivities. The interested reader must turn to the much more detailed collection of her writings (mentioned in the Epilogue) to savour these and all the many other fascinating details of life in West Wicklow, as Elizabeth Smith saw it, during the eventful famine decade.

After the wedding celebrations were over, she wrote:

> Now Annie is gone, taken her new name and her new station and her new duties, and ours is to be no more her home. [Annie's new home was, in fact, Humphrystown House, only a few miles away.] But she is with us; she and he, and they are loving children to us, he is as much our son as she is our daughter ... I have laid it down as a rule never to advise them – never, that is, to offer them advice. Should they want it, they will ask it the more readily that it is not obtruded upon them. The French family politeness is too little followed among us, it may appear ceremonious but it is really well bred and prudent ....

* * *

Elizabeth closed her journal for the year 1850 on 31 December with this entry:

> Goodbye, old year. We are once more all together, though not exactly side by side, dear little Jack being at Russelstown [the nearby home of one of the Hornidge families]. A gloomy rainy Christmas it is, and windy some nights to that degree one almost fears the house may fall. James [King] and his two ladies [Annie and Jane] were up before day, breakfasted at a little after seven and then that active man walked off upon his own ten toes to catch the Bus in Blesinton. May be he won't stir up those two idle monkeys! Early risers all the Kings are; always in exercise he is. Annie will be enough out of doors at any rate; no fear of her getting ill for want of the open air. And they have no fires in their bedroom in the morning, just one to go warm to bed by and air their linen during the night. All very right; young people require none of these enervating luxuries, time enough for all such indulgence when years bring ailments along with them.
>
> It is very pleasant to see the Colonel so roused by this marriage.

Really he is quite an altered person, so gay, singing old hunting songs and mess ditties! No sleepiness, no fretfulness. Almost as young as he was ten years ago. Annie looks so happy too – and Janey – and Jack – and James, all do so well together.

Poor old over-anxious Mama had best determine to be happy too.

Smith/Grant Family Tree

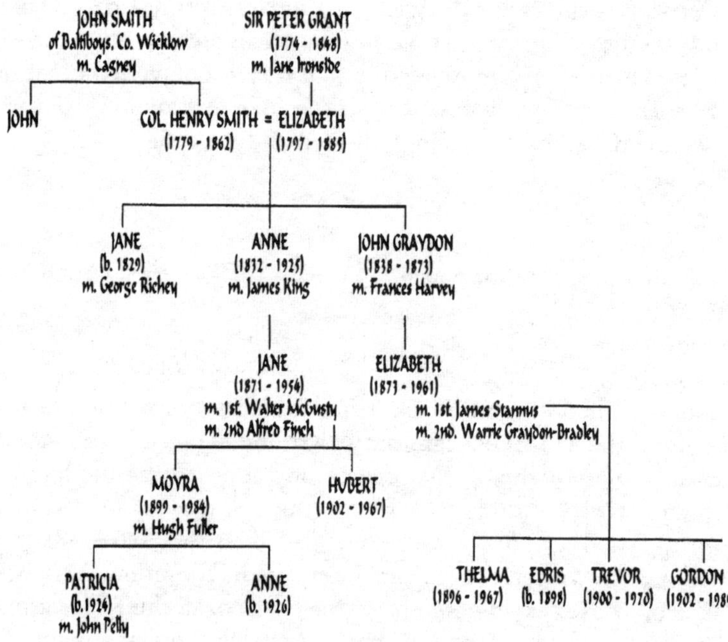

Family tree, showing the Smith connections with Edris Stannus (Ninette de Valois) and with Frances Pelly who co-edited The Highland Lady in Ireland

Epilogue

So ends Elizabeth Smith's journal of the famine decade though, happily, she was to continue writing her fascinating diary for many more years and plans to publish extracts from the remainder of her Irish journal are well advanced.

The years following 1850 saw great changes in Ireland, many of which resulted from the effects of the famine. The most startling was the huge drop in the population figures, especially among the poorest classes who had suffered most of all. But almost every other strata of society had also been affected, as Elizabeth Smith noted in 1849: 'The upper classes are now suffering, the farmer class a good deal, the landlord class a great deal'. That the farming class also suffered severely is evidenced by the disappearance at this time of one quarter of all farms (though a beneficial result arising from this was an increase in the average size of farms), while shopkeepers and traders, especially in rural areas, were badly affected too. Elizabeth's journal pointed out that when the contents of Manor Kilbride came up for sale towards the end of 1847, it was not the gentry who did the bidding but the middling farmers, and it was this class which more than others consolidated their position after the famine.

At the top of the social scale, many landlords were ruined and in a minority of cases this had resulted from their forbearance or benevolence towards their impoverished tenants. Ironically, there were instances where certain landlords who had been rendered bankrupt as a consequence of their benevolence, were succeeded in turn by new landlords whose first actions were to evict those very same tenants. After reading Elizabeth Smith's journal, it is not difficult to believe that the Baltiboys Estate might well have ended up in the lists of estates put into the hands of the receivers had Colonel Smith not had the good fortune to meet and marry this very talented woman.

Indeed the estate was greatly enlarged when Elizabeth, after the death of her husband, purchased land at Lacken with money left to her by her Aunt Bourne. Characteristically, one of the first things she did was to build a new school there, on which a commemorative stone bears her name to this day, and the teacher she installed was none other than the same Mr McDarby mentioned in her 1850 journal.

She often expressed concern about her own and her husband's health, and wrote about the fragility of life in general as well as the possibility that they might both die before their children had grown up. As she once expressed it: 'Shall I live to see these dear children men and women?' In fact, these fears turned out to be groundless because Colonel Smith, despite his chronic asthma, lived to be 83, and she attained the ripe old age of 88. They lie buried together under a flat tombstone in the shadow of St. Mary's church in Blessington – the tower of which is visible from Baltiboys – and buried with them is their son Jack, who died aged 35 in 1873.

* * *

Elizabeth mentioned several times that she and her husband and the children sometimes danced together at home in the evenings and also that Anne and Jane, their two daughters, were greatly in demand as dance partners as they grew older. For all that, Elizabeth could never, even in her wildest dreams, have foreseen that one of her great-granddaughters, Edris Stannus, also to be born at Baltiboys, would one day become an internationally-known ballet dancer and a world famous choreographer – better known, of course, by her stage name of Ninette de Valois.

In her autobiography, *Come Dance With Me*, Dame Ninette de Valois recalled her childhood memories of Baltiboys House, the stables, the farm bell, the gardens, the tall beech trees and the long avenue leading to a lodge at the entrance gates. She also recalled (and thus evoked some strange echoes of Elizabeth's journal) visiting and bringing gifts to the tenants' cottages dotted around the Baltiboys estate. In particular, she remembered her childhood visits to 'the home farm' about a mile away, where Kate Flanagan, the herdsman's wife, singled her out to teach her how to dance an Irish jig. Dame Ninette recorded in her book that had it not been for Mrs Flanagan's enterprise in persuading a little girl to stage her first dance performance on the stone floor of a County Wicklow farmhouse, she might never have turned to a career in ballet. She also recounted how her parents had made preparations to welcome their first-born child – a bonfire was laid on Baltiboys Hill and all was in readiness to ring the farmyard bell. However, when the baby turned out to be a girl instead of the expected boy, no bell was tolled nor was the bonfire lit.

The Smith connection with Baltiboys ended when Ninette's family sold the estate and went to live in England. She and her sister and two brothers were still quite young at the time and she did not see the old home again until 1957 when she was in Dublin with the Sadlers Wells

Elizabeth Smith is buried with her husband and son under a flat tombstone (left foreground) in St Mary's Churchyard, Blessington. (Dermot James)

Theatre Ballet. She did not pick an ideal time to view Baltiboys House. The day was overcast and wet and the house, once again awaiting sale to a new owner, was forlorn and almost empty except for a few remaining pieces of furniture which had been shrouded under sheets. By far the biggest change to meet her eyes was the scene all around the house which was now almost surrounded by Pollaphuca Reservoir, the waters of which drowned much of what she had remembered – including most of the long avenue leading from the house to the gate lodge. Many of the tenant cottages, familiar fields, most of the beech woods – and even the direct road to Blessington across Burgage Bridge – had disappeared beneath the waters in 1940.

For most people who know the area today, the huge artificial lake greatly enhances the scene, especially when viewed looking towards the backdrop of the Wicklow Mountains, or from the higher summits in the area, Mullaghcleevaun, Moanbane or Black Hill. Even from the very modest top of Baltiboys Hill, there is a comparatively little-known view of the whole area around Baltiboys now almost surrounded by the waters of the huge artificial lake. For all that, it is not difficult to appreciate why, on her brief return, Dame Ninette was greatly depressed and even thought that the scene resembled, as she expressed it, the last act of *The Cherry Orchard.*

It is tempting to speculate what Elizabeth Smith would think if she, too, could return to her beloved Baltiboys. Of course she would regret much of what has changed, as many of the older people living in the area still do, but surely this most practical woman would also take the view that the virtual absence of (to use a word so often used in her journal) *wretchedness* more than compensates for whatever else that has since disappeared.

* * *

After reading these pages, readers may wish to read the much more detailed extracts from the Irish journal of Elizabeth Smith which are already in print. This present volume represents only a very small selection taken from the many hundreds of entries appearing in *The Highland Lady in Ireland* edited by Patricia Pelly and Andrew Tod, published by the Canongate Press, Edinburgh. Permission to publish a selection of extracts in this volume has been generously given by the two editors and by the publishers, whose previously published volume of extracts from Elizabeth Smith's Scottish Memoirs[1] has contributed largely to her being very well known there. The decision by the Edinburgh publishers to produce a book based on extracts from her *Irish* journal was a remarkably enlightened

1. *Memoirs of a Highland Lady,* edited by Andrew Tod, Canongate Classics, Edinburgh, 1988.

one and deserves a much wider recognition here in Ireland than it has so far received. Plans are in hand to publish extracts from the remainder of Elizabeth Smith's Irish journal in the autumn of 1997 and a book based on her journal written when the family lived in France during 1843-44 is due for publication around the same time as this volume.

Appendix 1

Memorials of the Dead

Elizabeth Smith was born in Edinburgh in 1797, 17 years after her husband was born at Baltiboys. She died in 1885, having survived him by 25 years and she also survived her son Jack by 12 years. She and her husband and son lie buried together in the churchyard of St. Mary's in Blessington, and around them are to be found the tombstones of a number of their neighbours mentioned in the journal. The inscription on the Smith tombstone reads:

In Memory of
MAJOR GENERAL HENRY SMITH
Indian Army, of Baltiboys in this County
died the 27th December 1862
Aged 83 years
Erected by his son JOHN GRAYDON SMITH
Also to
JOHN GRAYDON SMITH
late Capt. 7th Royal Fusiliers
Son of the above
who died deeply regretted
the 3rd November 1873
Aged 35
"Not lost but gone before"
Also of ELIZABETH, Mother of the above
wife of
MAJOR GENERAL HENRY SMITH
and daughter of
SIR JOHN PETER GRANT
of Rothiemurchus, N.B.
died on the 14th November 1885
Aged 88

As already noted, Elizabeth Smith almost invariably referred to her husband as 'the Colonel', although the inscription on his tomb gives his rank as

Major General, indicating that the promotion came later. It was in this connection that Elizabeth Smith made a journal entry in 1849 about her husband having just then made 'a curious discovery'. This was that he had been a full Colonel ever since 1829 though, as she put it 'only gazetted now', adding that 'it is an unusual thing to promote retired officers... The Colonel only retired in 1835, he was then – unknown to himself – a Colonel of six years standing. Quare, is he not entitled to the encreased pay of his rank since 1835; he ought look into thi' Incidentally, the initials 'N.B.' after the word Rothiemurchus stand for North Britain, an old (English) name for Scotland.

Immediately alongside the Smith grave there are three irregular headstones, the first of which is inscribed in lovely old lettering: 'Of such is the Kingdom of Heaven' but, curiously, bearing no other inscription. This marks the grave of the Smith's third daughter, Elizabeth, who died of whooping cough, aged three months.

To the left of this is a second headstone erected by Thomas and Mary Gardiner over the grave of their five and a half year old daughter Annie who died at Baltiboys in 1836. It appears that this was Elizabeth's niece, the daughter of her sister Mary, whose husband Thomas had advised the Smiths to go to France for a couple of years in 1843.

The third headstone in this group bears the following inscription:

In Remembrance of
JAMES KING ESQ
late clerk of the beagles
in the County Fermanagh
son of
JOHN KING ESQ
and CHARLOTTE TOTTENHAM his wife
who died at Baltiboys on the 24th Janry 1879

This James King was the husband of Elizabeth's younger daughter Annie, whom he married in 1850.

A short distance away, enclosed within railings, are three graves of the Leeson family who lived at Russborough, including Joseph, the third Earl of Milltown who, as Elizabeth frequently noted, was an inveterate gambler and who died in 1866. His son Edward mentioned by Elizabeth in her description of the drive to Glendalough -and who succeeded as the fifth earl, is buried alongside.

There are several Hornidge headstones including one in memory of Richard Hornidge of Russelstown (1822–1887), and his brother John James Hornidge (1821–1889). Elizabeth described their father, John, as 'Hal's oldest friend, the gay companion of his younger days'. When he died in 1847, she wrote that the funeral took place on 'a bright sunny day such as the old man used to enjoy when driving along ... glancing a proud eye as he passed in his high phaeton over the Russellstown woods and meadows covered with the cattle he had such pleasure in calculating the profits on.'

Also in the churchyard is a headstone marking the grave of Capt. Edward Stuart Hornidge, OBE., of Tulfarris (1887-1965) and his second wife, Thelma (née Stannus) who was born at Baltiboys and was a grand-daughter of Elizabeth Smith. It was she who accompanied her sister Edris, better known as Ninette de Valois, when the latter revisited Baltiboys House in !957. Thelma died in 1967.

No headstone appears to exist here for Tom Darker, the Baltiboys steward, nor for any of the other members of that family named in the journal. Another Darker, James Darker of Burgage Cottage and his wife Deborah, who were contemporaries of Elizabeth,. are buried in the churchyard. The headstone which marks their grave appears to bear a 'misprint' as it records that his wife died in 1881 aged 84, and that he died at the age of 90 in '1801'.

* * *

A few miles away, in the prettily situated Kilbride churchyard at Cloghleagh, there is a memorial to various members of the Finnamore family who lived at Ballyward during Elizabeth's time. The lettering is difficult to decipher but one of the members of the family interred here was John Finnamore who, when he died in 1849, was described by her – as 'the Colonel's last yeoman friend'.

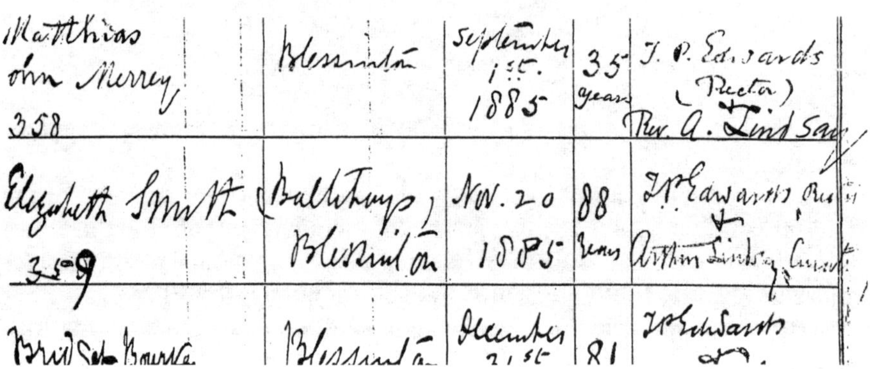

Matthias John Merrey 358	Blessington	September 1st 1885	35 years	J. P. Edwards (Rector) Rev. A. Lindsay
Elizabeth Smith 359	Baltiboys, Blessington	Nov. 20 1885	88 years	J P Edwards Rector, Arthur Lindsay, Curate
Bridget Bourke	Blessington	December 21st	81	J P Edwards

The entry for Elizabeth Smith in the Burial Register at St Mary's Church, Blessington.

Appendix 2

Historical and Topographical Descriptions

Samuel Lewis' Topographical Dictionary was published in 1837, six years after Colonel Henry Smith has returned with Elizabeth from India. He was at that time in the process of rebuilding Baltiboys House and had erected the new school nearby, both of which are mentioned in the following extracts.

BLESSINGTON, (St. Mary) or BURGAGE is a market and post-town, and a parish in the barony of Lower Talbotstown, county of Wicklow, and the province of Leinster ... containing with Burgage 2677 inhabitants, of which number 426 are in the town. It consists of one long main street and contains about 50 houses, which are mostly of respectable appearance, and a good inn or hotel. Considerable improvement has taken place since the construction of the new turnpike road from Dublin to Carlow, by way of Baltinglass, in 1829, by which the Waterford mail and the Kilkenny day mail and several coaches and cars to the counties of Wexford and Carlow, have been brought through it ....

The market is on Thursday; and Fairs are held on May 12th, July 5th and Nov. 12th. Here is a station of the constabulary police, and the residence of the chief officer of the peace preservation forces resides in the town, The inhabitants were incorporated by the charter of the 21st of Chas. II (1669) granted by the Archbishop of Dublin and Chancellor of Ireland ....

The parish, which prior to the erection of the town and church in 1683, was called Burgage, comprising 15,570 statute acres, The land is chiefly under tillage and pasturage, and there are some large tracts of mountain waste, on which there are turf bogs; the state of agriculture has considerably improved ....

The Marquis of Downshire has a handsome mansion and demesne of 410 statute acres, with a deer park of 240 acres, all surrounded by a wall and situated on the right of the road from Dublin. The mansion was originally built by Primate Boyle, the last ecclesiastical chancellor of Ireland, who held his court of chancery here and built houses for the six clerks, two of which remain; the interior was burnt by the insurgents in 1798 and has not been restored; the demesne has been richly embellished with fine timber.

About two miles from the town, on the road to Baltinglass, is Russborough, the elegant seat of the Earl of Milltown; the mansion erected after a design by Mr Cassels, and consists of a centre and two wings, connected by semicircular colonnades of alternated Ionic and Corinthian pillars, and presenting a noble facade of hewn stone 700 feet in extent; the interior is fitted up in a style of sumptuous magnificence; the floors of the principal apartments are of polished mahogany and there is an extensive and valuable collection of paintings, chiefly of the Italian school, arranged in seven apartments appropriated to its reception; the demesne comprises 405 statute acres tastefully laid out and planted. Russellstown, the seat of J. Hornidge. Esq., is also in the parish ....

In the R.C. divisions, this parish is partly in that of Blackditches, and partly in that of Ballymore Eustace, the first union comprises also the parishes of Rathmore, Kilbride and Kilteel, and contains three chapels, situated at Cross and Eadestown, in Rathmore and in Kilbride ....

There are some ruins of the old church of Burgage and in the churchyard are the remains of a castle and on the outside is a very fine cross, hewn out of one very large block of granite, and about 14 feet high .... Blessington gave the title of an earl to the family of Gardiner, now extinct; and Russborough gave the inferior titles of Viscount and baron to the Earl of Milltown.

BOYSTOWN, or BALTIBOYS, a parish, in the barony of Lower Talbotstown, county of Wicklow, and province of Leinster, 3 miles (s.) from Blessington; containing 3235 inhabitants. This parish is situated on the Liffey and King's rivers and comprises, with the chapelries of Granabeg and Kilbeg about 20,000 statute acres, of which, nearly two thirds are in mountain, and the remainder is chiefly pasture land with a small portion under tillage. The system of agriculture is improving; there is a tract of bog called Ballynahowen, near Blackditches. At Baltiboys is a good quarry of slate, which was formerly worked to advantage, but is at present discontinued; and there are quarries of granite at Ballyknockan, which are still in operation. The surrounding scenery is bold and mountainous, and there are several gentlemen's seats, among them are Tulfarris, the seat of R. Hornidge, Esq., which was partly burned by the insurgents in 1798; Baltiboys, of Lieut. Col. Smith, who has recently erected a handsome mansion on the demesne, which commands some, fine and extensive views; Humphrystown, of W. Cotton, Esq., the demesne which is tastefully laid out and planted; Willmount, of W. Dunravin, Esq., from which also there is a fine view, including the mansion and demesne of Russborough. There are also two shooting lodges, one at Kilbeg, belonging to W. Brady, Esq., and one at Marlfield, the property of Richard LaTouche, Esq.

It is a vicarage, in diocese of Dublin, and is part of the union of St. Mary's Blessington or Burgage .... In the R.C. division, it is included in the union or district of Blackditches, which comprises the whole of this parish and a part of Blessington; there are chapels at Blackditches and in the small village of Lacken, both of which are in this parish, A schoolhouse, with apartments for a master and mistress, was built at the expense of Lieut. Col. Smyth [sic], there are eight hedge schools, in which are about 145 boys and 114 girls. There was an ancient cemetery at Baltiboys, and another at Templepooda.

BALLYMORE or BALLYMORE-EUSTACE, a market town and parish in the barony of Lower Talbotstown, containing 2085 inhabitants, of which number 841 are in the town, It is situated on the river Liffey, over which is a handsome bridge of six arches, and consists of one principal and three smaller streets; there is a penny post to Naas.

The great southern road formerly passed through it, but it has been diverted through the village of Kilcullen by the construction of a new line, and the town has since considerably decayed. A large manufactory, in which every description of cloth is made, was erected in the vicinity by Mr Christopher Drumgoole in 1802, and when in full work, employs about 700 persons.

The parish is the head of a lordship and manor belonging to the Archbishops of Dublin and comprising the parishes of Ballymore, Ballybrought, Cotlandstown, Yagoe, Tipperkevin, and Tubber, in the county of Dublin, and of Milltown and Tornant, and part of Rathsallagh, in the county of Wicklow. The system of agriculture is improving.

Mount Cashel Lodge, the property of the earl of Mount Cashel, is pleasantly situated, and is in the occupation of Mr Drumgoole, The principal residences are Artinode, that of E. Holmes, Esq.; Season, of Mrs O'Brien; and Willfield, of R. Doyle, Esq.

The church is a plain building with an embattled tower surmounted with pinnacles, erected in 1820 at a cost of £900; the churchyard is of great extent, and contains the remains of an old church, and numerous ancient tombstones. In the R.C. division ... the chapel at Ballymore is a substantial and commodious building, and there is another at Hollywood ....

About a mile from the town, the Liffey forms the celebrated cascade of Poul-a-phuca, or the Demon's Hole, consisting of three consecutive waterfalls 150 feet in height. The chasm is only forty feet wide and is skirted on each side by perpendicular masses of granwacke rock; and when the river is swollen by heavy rains the water rushes down with such tumultuous impetuosity into a circular basin of the rock, worn quite smooth and of great depth, the form of which imparts to it the motion of a whirlpool, and from which the cascade derives its name ....

Immediately above the basin, on the line of the new turnpike road from Blessington to Baltinglass, is a picturesque bridge of one pointed arch springing from rock to rock built in an antique style from a design by the late Alex. Nimmo, Esq., at an expense, including the land arches and approaches, of £4,074.15, the span of the arch is 47 feet and the height of the keystone of the arch above the bed of the river is 150 feet.

The late Earl of Milltown took a lively interest in this spot, which he enhanced by planting on one side of the glen forming part of his estate, making walks, and erecting rustic bridges in various places, besides a banqueting room, 45 feet long by 25 feet wide, from which there is a delightful view of the falls and the bridge ... but owing to the disturbances of 1798 he went abroad, and some time after sold it to Col. Aylmer, who is now the proprietor, and has appointed a person to take proper care of it, by whom accommodation has been prepared for the numerous visitors that resort hither from Dublin and elsewhere ....

Index

Index to place names

Index to persons

1. Note: *References in the text to the Smith family of Baltiboys are so numerous that they have not been indexed.*